USING POETRY

KEY STAGE 2 Y3–4
P4–5

FRANCES MACKAY

Contents

Published by Hopscotch Educational Publishing Ltd,
Unit 2, The Old Brushworks, 56 Pickwick Road,
Corsham, SN13 9BX (Tel: 01249 701701)

© 1999 Hopscotch Educational Publishing

Written by Frances Mackay
Foreword by Wes Magee
Series design by Blade Communications
Illustrated by Susan Hutchison
Cover illustration by Susan Hutchison
Printed by Clintplan, Southam

Frances Mackay hereby asserts her moral right to be identified
as the author of this work in accordance with the Copyright,
Designs and Patents Act, 1988.

ISBN 1-902239-13-X

 **ABOUT THE SERIES**

Developing Literacy Skills is a series of books aimed at developing key literacy skills using stories, non-fiction, poetry and rhyme, spelling and grammar, from Key Stage 1 (P1–3) through to Key Stage 2 (P4–7).

The series offers a structured approach which provides detailed lesson plans to teach specific literacy skills. A unique feature of the series is the provision of differentiated photocopiable activities aimed at considerably reducing teacher preparation time. Suggestions for using the photocopiable pages as a stimulus for further work in the classroom are provided to ensure maximum use of this resource.

ABOUT THIS BOOK

This book is for teachers of children at Key Stage 2 Y3–4 and Scottish levels P4–5. It aims to:

✦ develop children's literacy skills through exposure to and experience of a wide range of stimulating poetry with supporting differentiated activities which are both diversified and challenging;
✦ support teachers by providing practical teaching methods based on whole-class, group, paired and individual teaching;
✦ encourage enjoyment and curiosity as well as developing skills of interpretation and response.

 **CHAPTER CONTENT**

◆ Overall aims

These outline the aims for both lessons set out in each chapter.

◆ Featured poems

This lists the poems that are used in the lessons together with the page number on which a photocopiable version of the poem can be found.

 **Intended learning**

This sets out the specific aims for each individual lesson within the chapter.

◆ Starting point

This provides ideas for introducing the activity and may include key questions to ask the children.

◆ Group activities

This explains the task(s) the children will carry out in the lesson without supporting photocopiable activities.

◆ Using the differentiated activity sheets

This explains how to use each sheet as well as providing guidance on the type of child who will benefit most from each sheet.

◆ Plenary session

This suggests ideas for whole-class sessions to discuss the learning outcomes and follow-up work.

◆ Using the photocopiable sheets as a stimulus for further work

This is a useful list of further activities that can be developed from the activity sheets. These ideas maximise the use of the photocopiable pages.

◆ Other ideas for using...

This contains other ideas for developing the skills explored in each chapter. The ideas will have completely different learning intentions from the featured lessons and provide a range of alternatives.

USING THE POETRY PAGES

For shared reading, the poems on these pages could be enlarged by hand or on the photocopier. Alternatively each child or pair could have their own photocopy.

Foreword

Wes Magee, a well-known poet who provides popular in-school sessions on teaching poetry, explains the level of poetry and related activities that children should be addressing at this age. He also gives several examples of different types of poetry which will prove a useful introduction to a topic sometimes seen as 'difficult to do' with primary school children.

Years 3 and 4 children should be well beyond nursery rhymes and verse for the very young. They will have experienced hearing poetry read aloud by teachers (parents too, it is hoped) and be able to read poems themselves. The many, many well illustrated books currently available mean that children should not be missing out on a regular diet of poems both old and new.

It is useful if children learn to name parts when it comes to understanding poems. They should become familiar with and able to identify the following: title, verse, stanza, structure (or form) and chorus.

Title – The name of the poem. A title often acts as a doorway into the poem. It introduces the poem's subject matter and offers a strong clue about what is to follow. (For example, Clement Clarke Moore's 'A Visit from St. Nicholas'.)

Verse – This is a group of lines within a poem. A poem can be a single verse, or it can contain many verses (such as the 21 verses in Allan Ahlberg's long poem, 'The Mighty Slide'). A stanza is an alternative term for 'verse'.

Structure (or form) – This is the way in which a poem is constructed (for example, in verses). It has a visual aspect on the page, and children need to understand that poems have different forms. Some structures/forms are well known and long standing, like sonnets, limericks, syllable counts, or shape on the page.

Chorus – A refrain (often set out as a separate verse) repeated at intervals throughout the poem. This is the part children learn easily and like to chant during an out-loud reading.

 Rhythm

Reading poems aloud (either by the teacher, or by the children themselves) is a surer way of appreciating (i.e. hearing) rhythm. Some poems are not especially musical, the poet preferring to concentrate on expressions of feeling, or the language of description, but many poems do contain rhythm and beat.

Rhythm (as in songs and hymns) has infinite variations. It can be simple and repetitive, or complex. In the following poem we see a simple rhythm that is repeated in subsequent verses. There are two 'beats' per line. The pattern of syllable counts per line (6/5/6/5) helps to emphasise the chanting tone.

> *Andrew Flag plays football,*
> *Jane swings on the bars,*
> *'Chucker' Peach climbs drainpipes,*
> *Spike is seeing stars.*

In the next example we 'hear' more complex rhythms. The beat changes as the reader proceeds down the page. Note, too, the poem's shape. It is repeated in verses 2 and 3. The line indentations are visual clues for the reader; they indicate changes in line length and rhythm. It is also well worth spending a moment examining the rhyme scheme. It is quite complicated! – a/a/b/c/b/c/a/a/-/-/a.

> *Up on the Downs,*
> *Up on the Downs,*
> *A skylark flutters*
> *And the fox barks shrill.*
> *Brown rabbit scutters*
> *And the hawk hangs still.*
> *Up on the Downs,*
> *Up on the Downs,*
> *With butterflies*
> *jigging like*
> *costumed clowns.*

 Rhyme

Rhyme is to poem, as boiled egg is to egg cup. They work together and should fit snugly. Poems, of course, do <u>not</u> have to rhyme (for example,

Longfellow's 'The Song of Hiawatha'), but more often than not they do. As with rhythm, poets have used their ingenuity to invent innumerable rhyme variations. As in the case of rhythm, rhyme schemes can be simple or more complex.

The following is a simply rhymed couplet:

> *On Monday icy rains poured down*
> *and flooded drains all over town.*

(Note the instance of internal rhyme – rains/drains.)

Here, by way of contrast, is a verse displaying a more sophisticated use of rhyme:

> Has someone told? And if so, <u>who</u>?
> I sit on the hard bench outside
> the Head's room, and I'm in a stew.
> See me now, the message said.
> Time's dragging. I wish I was dead.
> Has someone told? And if so <u>who</u>?

A pupil (boy or girl?) worries as he/she waits to see the headteacher. A guilty conscience gnawing away? Trouble in store? The subject matter is one thing: the use of rhyme another. The first line is repeated at the end of the verse (like a chorus or refrain) and 'who' is rhymed with 'stew' at the end of the third line. Then there is a rhymed couplet towards the end

of the verse – said/dead. The second line does not rhyme. Line indentations not only give the verse its distinctive shape on the page but also underscore the use of rhyme.

The poet's versifying techniques (the rhymes, the rhythms) only truly come alive if the poem is read aloud – more than once. Unlike a long story with its strong narrative flow, poems benefit from repeated readings. It is only then that children (and teachers) fully understand the written communication and appreciate the rhymes and rhythms. Too often poems are scanned just once and rejected as dull, boring or incomprehensible. Unlike a story, the language used in poems can be denser. Repeated readings are required!

<u>R</u>epeated <u>r</u>eadings <u>r</u>equired – that is an example of alliteration, an effective writing mechanism. It occurs when writers use a sequence of words beginning with the same letter.

> *Sharma and Shoha and Sancho*
> *heard the swish of the surf,*
> *sniffed the sweet scent of seaweed,*
> *and stared at shrimps*
> *shifting in still pools.*

That is alliteration almost done to death, but at least it's easy to spot! In the shape poem below, 'A Giant Rocket', the alliteration (using letters 's' and 'd') is less obvious but just as effective.

Using Poetry
KS2: Y3–4/P4–5

Developing
Literacy
Skills

© Hopscotch Educational Publishing

5

Structure

Children can further understand poetry by learning to identify simple forms (or structures). It will also help their own writing. We know only too well the outcome when we ask children to "write a poem". Rhyme, usually in a doggerel (i.e. trivial) style, will tend to dominate the subject matter. Teachers are all too familiar with:

> *I like my cat*
> *It sits on the mat*
> *It likes doing that*
> *It caught a bat*
> *and it ate my hat*
> *It looks like a rat...' and so on...*

There is, one has to admit, a certain surreal humour at play here but mostly the piece is banal. <u>Everything</u> has gone into the rhymes: <u>nothing</u> into the subject matter.

By reading and learning about a few poetic forms, children will have definite and understood structures upon which to base their own writings. Three fairly simple structures are examined below.

'Character Poem' using a triple rhyme

This kind of poem paints a simple picture (in words) of a person – such as a teacher, footballer, knight in armour, mountaineer or a lady pirate...

> *This pirate had no beard at all,*
> *pink chin smooth as a marble hall*
> *and voice clear as a robin's call.*
>
> *This pirate strange with big brown eyes*
> *and flowing hair and sudden sighs*
> *The truth? A woman... in disguise!*

With two equal verses, each has three lines that rhyme. This is known as a tercet.

Acrostic

Another simple poetry form is the acrostic. The title (such as 'Christmas') is written vertically down the page and each initial letter is used to begin a line of writing. By using rhymed couplets the poem takes on a greater element of rhythm.

> <u>C</u> arols drift across the night
> <u>H</u> olly gleams by candlelight
> <u>R</u> oaring fire, a spooky tale
> <u>I</u> ce and snow and wind and hail.
> <u>S</u>
> <u>T</u>
> <u>M</u>
> <u>A</u>
> <u>S</u>

Some acrostics have the title word in the middle of the poem, or even at the end. Once they are aware of the structure (and the term) children will readily spot acrostics in poetry anthologies and can then attempt to write their own versions.

Haiku

The haiku is a simple non-rhymed poetry structure but is slightly more difficult than it looks. The haiku has been around for many centuries (it started life on the Far East), and is short, and ultra concise. It has a mathematical basis:

Three lines...

Line 1: 5 syllables
Line 2: 7 syllables
Line 3: 5 syllables

There is no rhyme. The idea is to make a complete communication in just 17 syllables. Again, if children read plenty of haiku (there are lots published in anthologies) they will quickly pick up the idea.

They will need to be taught about syllables. Use mouth shape or separate sounds to describe them, and then let the children <u>speak</u> examples of one syllable words (me, go, home, dog), two syllable

words (captain, butter, elbow, painting), three syllable words (yesterday, butterfly, astronaut), and so on.

Let the children count the syllables in a published haiku:

Fox

*Slinks to the wood's edge
and – with one paw raised – surveys
the open meadows*

The syllable pattern is 5 – 7 – 5.

These are just three examples of simple poetic forms – the triple rhymed verse (tercet), the acrostic, and the haiku. There are dozens of others.

It all goes to demonstrate that the terms 'poem' and 'poetry' cover a vast range of varied written communication. It is important that while children grow increasingly aware of diversity in poetry they never lose the ability to simply <u>enjoy</u> reading poems and hearing them read by teachers and parents.

At this age (Years 3 and 4), young minds are wide open to the rich language and exciting rhythms offered by poems both old and new.

Wes Magee is a former primary school teacher and headteacher. He has been a full-time author since 1989. For information on his services for schools, telephone 01751 417633.

Acknowledgements

The author and publisher gratefully acknowledge permission to reproduce copyright material in this book.

'Balloon' by Colleen Thibaudeau. Reprinted by permission of the author.

'Winter' by Judith Nicholls from *Midnight Forest*, reprinted by permission of Faber & Faber Ltd.

'When Skies are Low and Days are Dark' by N M Bodecker from *Snowman Sniffles* © 1983 N M Bodecker. Reprinted by permission of Faber & Faber Ltd.

'Winter Morning' by Ogden Nash from *Collected Poems of Ogden Nash*, copyright © 1961 Ogden Nash, renewed. Reprinted by permission of Curtis Brown Ltd.

'Week of Winter Weather' by Wes Magee © 1981 Wes Magee. Reprinted by permission of the author.

'Roots Man' by Grace Walker Gordon. Reprinted by permission of the author.

'Childhood Tracks' (p11, 22 lines) by James Berry from *Playing a Dazzler* (Hamish Hamilton, 1996), © 1996 James Berry. Reproduced by permission Penguin Books Ltd.

'Mary, Mary' by Max Fatchen from *Wry Rhymes for Troublesome Times*, published by Penguin Books Ltd. Copyright © 1983 Max Fatchen. Reproduced by permission of John Johnson (Author's Agent) Ltd.

'The Loch Ness Monster's Song' by Edwin Morgan © Edwin Morgan from *Poems of Thirty Years*, Carcanet, Manchester, 1982. Reprinted by permission of Carcanet Press Ltd.

'Granny' by Spike Milligan from *Silly Verses for Kids*. Reprinted by permission of Spike Milligan Productions Ltd.

'The Ghoul' by Jack Prelutsky from *Nightmares, Poems to Trouble Your Sleep*, by Jack Prelutsky. Reprinted by permission of A&C Black.

'The Snitterjipe' by James Reeves © James Reeves from *The Wandering Moon and Other Poems* (Puffin Books) by James Reeves. Reprinted by permission of the James Reeves Estate.

'The Sloojee' by Colin West. Reprinted by permission of the author.

'The Fly' by Walter de la Mare from *The Complete Poems of Walter de la Mare*, 1969 (USA: 1970). Reprinted by permission of the Literary Trustees of Walter de la Mare and the Society of Authors as their representative.

'The Stag' by Ted Hughes from *Season Songs*. Reprinted by permission of Faber & Faber Ltd.

'Down Behind the Dustbin' (p41, 36 lines) by Michael Rosen from *You Tell Me* by Roger McGough and Michael Rosen (Kestrel, 1979). Copyright © Michael Rosen, 1979. Reproduced by permission of Penguin Books Ltd.

Every effort has been made to trace the owners of copyright of poems in this book and the publisher apologises for any inadvertent omissions. Any persons claiming copyright for any material should contact the publisher who will be happy to pay the permissions fees requested and who will amend the information in this book on any subsequent reprint.

Observational poems

Overall aims

- To compare different views of the same subject.
- To discuss poets' choice of words and phrases that describe and create impact.
- To collect suitable words and phrases in order to write a poem.
- To explore adjectives and synonyms.

Featured poems (page 56)

Winter Morning by Ogden Nash
Winter by Judith Nicholls
Week of Winter Weather by Wes Magee
When Skies are Low and Days are Dark by N M Bodecker

LESSON ONE

Intended learning

- To compare different views of the same subject.
- To discuss the poets' choice of words and phrases that describe and create impact.

Starting point: Whole class

- Ask the children to tell you what they feel about winter. Do they like this season? What words would they use to describe it? Tell them that they will now find out what other people think about winter by sharing some poems written about it.
- Ask them to follow the words of each poem on page 56 as you read them. For each poem, briefly discuss the children's responses to it. Does the poet seem to like or dislike winter? What tells you this? Which poem do the children personally like best? Can they say why?
- Ask the children to tell you how different the approach to the subject of winter is in the poems 'Winter Morning' and 'When Skies are Low and Days are Dark'. Compare the words and phrases used – how the first poem uses happy, more light-hearted images, such as 'Turning tree

stumps into snowmen and houses into birthday cakes'. Does one poem make you feel cold, just by reading it? Why?

Group activities

- Ask the children to work in pairs or small groups to carry out the following tasks:
a) underline one sentence or line from each poem which sums up the feeling of the whole poem;
b) for each poem, write two lists – one list containing words/phrases used to describe winter and another list containing words/phrases used to describe things the winter weather does;
c) select a word or phrase from each poem which creates a strong image in your mind;
d) write down ideas about how the poem 'Winter' differs from all the other poems.

Plenary session

Ask some groups to read out the line they have chosen which best sums up the feeling of each poem. Why have they chosen this line? Have others chosen the same line? Could the title be the best line for 'Week of Winter Weather'? Why was it harder to select just one line in this poem?

Compare the lists of words and phrases to describe winter and how we feel. Remind the children about adjectives. How many of their chosen words are adjectives? Compare the lines chosen that create impact. Why have they selected these lines?

Discuss the personification used in 'Winter' – such as how winter 'creeps' and 'prowls' like a person might. Why do the children think the poet has used this approach? Discuss other uses of imagery, such as metaphor – 'Winter is the king of showmen' – and simile – 'frost bites like a hungry shark'. Why do they think these images have been used? How do the images help the poem?

Observational poems

◆ LESSON TWO ◆

◆ Intended learning

✦ To explore adjectives and synonyms.
✦ To collect suitable words and phrases in order to write a poem using a particular pattern.

◆ Starting point: Whole class

✦ Remind the children about the poems explored in Lesson One. Explain that each poet has made his or her own observations about winter and how it feels to them. They have used words and phrases that relate to our senses. Ask the children to explore this further by finding references to the senses in each of the poems – do the words/phrases relate to something we can see? Smell? Touch/feel? Hear or taste? Which sense is most represented? Which one the least? What might be the reasons for this? Would poems on a different subject, say food, for example, have a greater bias to other senses such as smell and taste?

✦ Write the following lines on the board:
  'Smooth and clean and frost white',
  'Winter raced down the frozen stream',
  'Saturday's sky was ghostly grey' and
  'When skies are low and days are dark'.
Tell the children that many of the words in these sentences are adjectives. Ask them to tell you what adjectives are and then to find them in the sentences. Discuss the fact that some words can be used as a verb or an adjective, depending on the way it is used in a sentence. Use the word 'clean' to illustrate this point. Could any other words in these sentences be used as both a verb and an adjective? Make sure the children understand the term 'adjective' before continuing.

✦ Challenge the children to think of other adjectives they could use in the sentences and still retain the original meaning. What could be another word for 'smooth', 'clean' and so on? Remind them that words that have the same meaning are called synonyms and that a thesaurus can be useful in finding these words. Explain that the poets themselves may use this type of dictionary in order to find better words to use when they are editing their initial drafts of a poem. Use a thesaurus with the children to find synonyms for some of the adjectives in the sentences. Point out that the meaning of the word must be the same.

✦ Tell them that they will now have an opportunity to explore adjectives and synonyms by writing their own senses poem about winter. Explain that each group will be exploring a different form of poetry and that they will be following a particular pattern in their poems. Model the patterns then briefly brainstorm some possible subject ideas.

◆ Using the differentiated activity sheets

Activity sheet 1

This activity provides a lot of support. It requires the children to write a simple poem using adjectives.

Activity sheet 2

This activity uses an adaptation of cinquains. The children are required to use adjectives as well as a relating phrase to produce their poem.

Activity sheet 3

This activity is more challenging in that it requires the children to use alliterative adjectives to describe the subject.

◆ Plenary session

Ask someone from each group to explain the pattern they used in their poem. Share some of the poems to illustrate the pattern. Discuss whether using a set pattern helps or hinders the writing of a poem. Did they use a thesaurus or dictionary to help them find the 'best' adjective to use? Ask if someone would like to improve one of their poems further (or use a poem from the sheets) and model how to use the thesaurus to find more expressive/appropriate adjectives.

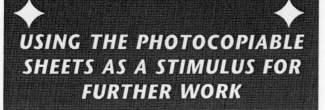

Observational poems

USING THE PHOTOCOPIABLE SHEETS AS A STIMULUS FOR FURTHER WORK

✦ Ask the children to use the same poetry pattern to write observational poems on other subjects.

✦ Make a large wall display of 'Winter adjectives', starting with adjectives from the children's poems. Challenge the children to add to the display over several days or weeks. Display the poems near the word wall.

✦ Make a class dictionary of adjectives, beginning with the words on the activity sheets. Encourage the children to refer to the dictionary for their creative writing.

✦ Have races to find adjectives in dictionaries, newspapers and books. Who can find an adjective that begins with 'b'? Who can find an adjective that could describe a house?

✦ Ask the children to find other poems about winter in anthologies. Make a class book of their favourite ones.

✦ Explore antonyms by writing summer poems! Replace the words in winter poems with summer alternatives.

✦ Explore alliteration further. Who can write the longest sentence about winter using alliteration?

✦ Make wall charts of synonyms for reference purposes. Begin with commonly over-used words such as 'nice' and 'good'. Encourage the children to refer to the charts when writing stories or reports.

OTHER IDEAS FOR USING OBSERVATIONAL POEMS

✦ Ask the children to paint pictures to capture the senses/feelings created by a poem, then to write words/ phrases that sum up these feelings.

✦ Make popcorn. The children should write words to describe the things they see, taste, smell, touch and hear during the cooking and eating. Use these words to make group or individual popcorn poems.

✦ Ask the children to find poems that relate to particular senses. Make a collection of 'listening poems' or 'tasty poems', for example.

✦ Put an object into a 'feely bag'. Ask the children to say words to describe the object. Use the words to make a class poem. Do not reveal the object until the poem is complete. How accurate were their descriptions/perceptions?

✦ Make simple senses poems by asking the children to complete sentences, for example:
'The nicest sight on a summer's day is...'
'I hate to touch...'
'The nicest smells are... and...'

✦ Find poems that explore people's feelings. Use them to discuss issues/concerns relevant to the children.

✦ Ask the children to find poems to 'cheer you up when you're sad', 'scare the daylights out of your brother' or 'help people understand me'. Explore ideas as to why the poems were written in the first place and how poems are often used as a way of expressing inner-most feelings and observations about daily life.

✦ Winter ✦

1 Read this poem. It has been written using an adjective for each of the senses.

sight	white
sound	quiet
touch	cold
taste	watery
smell	clean
subject	SNOW

2 We can improve the adjectives in the poem by using a thesaurus to find synonyms for each word.

sight	spotless
sound	silent
touch	freezing
taste	bland
smell	fresh
subject	SNOW

3 Look at the way this poem has been improved in the same way:

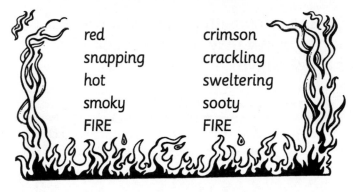

red	crimson
snapping	crackling
hot	sweltering
smoky	sooty
FIRE	FIRE

4 Write a senses poem of your own about winter. Use the word boxes and/or a thesaurus to help you.

sight _____

sound _____

touch _____

taste _____

smell _____

subject _____

Sight Words	Sound Words	Touch Words	Taste Words	Smell Words
bare	loud	soggy	bitter	fresh
tall	soft	dewy	sweet	earthy
grey	hissing	hard	dry	woody
bleak	lashing	soft	tasteless	clean
rosy	thunderous	warm	tangy	pure
round	noisy	cold	delicious	sweet
old	peaceful	damp	wet	musty
gloomy	calm	wet	scrumptious	pleasant
dull	howling	chilly	tasty	stale
sparkling	pounding	shivery	bland	smoky
bumpy	crackly	clammy	flavourless	lovely
dark		squelchy		refreshing
misty				

✦ Write some more poems on the back of this page.

✦ Winter ✦

✦ Read these two poems. They use an adaptation of a type of poem called a cinquain. They are set out like this:

1st line – one word, the subject

2nd line – two adjectives

3rd line – three adjectives

4th line – four words forming a phrase

Last line – one word, the subject

Snow,
spotless, new,
slushy, slippery, dangerous,
fun to slide in,
snow.

Winter,
cold, bitter,
biting, vicious, harsh,
seems to never end,
winter.

✦ Now write some poems of your own using the same pattern. Think of winter subjects to write about. The words in the box below may help you begin. To find more descriptive words, a thesaurus has synonyms for these words.

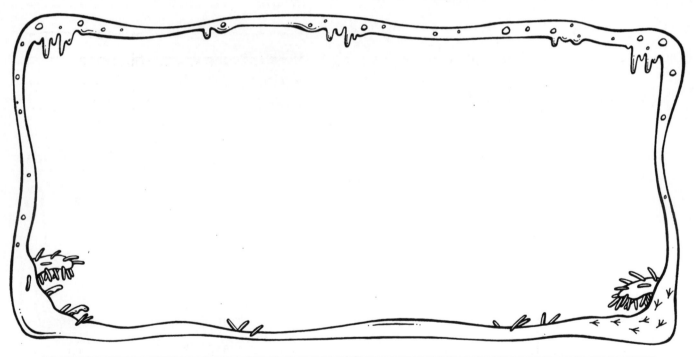

biting	leafless	bare	cold	bitter	misty	murky	gloomy
dull	frosty	chilly	icy	grey	whitish	howling	smoky
dark	soggy	sweet	fresh	clear	foggy	invigorating	

✦ Winter ✦

✦ Read these poems. They have a particular pattern to them:

1st line – a phrase using the senses (looks, feels, smells, sounds or tastes)

2nd line – adjective

3rd line – adjective

4th line – pronoun and adjective

Last line – adjective

✦ Notice that all the adjectives begin with the same letter (alliteration).

The moonlight on snow looks sparkling,
spectacular.
It's special,
satisfying.

The roaring fire feels welcoming,
warm.
It's wonderful,
worthwhile.

The violent storm sounds ferocious,
frightening.
It's fierce,
formidable.

✦ Use the same pattern to write some winter poems of your own. Think of a suitable subject and some descriptive words to describe it. Use a dictionary and a thesaurus to help you find adjectives that begin with the same letter. You may like to use some of the words in the box below.

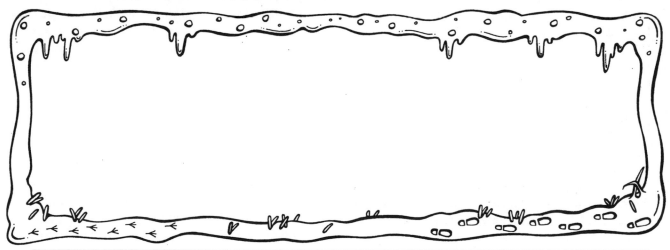

murky	mysterious	misty	mild	menacing	magical
dangerous	dreary	dusky	dull	draughty	dormant	dry
eerie	exhilarating	enjoyable	exhausting	earthy	extraordinary

Using Poetry

KS2: Y3–4/P4–5

Developing
literacy
skills

Photocopiable

© Hopscotch Educational Publishing

13

Shape poems

 Overall aims

✦ To read and share a range of shape poems.
✦ To discuss the effect of calligrams in poetry.
✦ To invent own calligrams.
✦ To select appropriate words and style of presentation in writing own shape poem.

 Featured poems (page 57)

Balloon by Colleen Thibaudeau
The Snail, **Oh To Be a Hexagon**, **Mouse** and **The Night-Time Monster** by Frances Mackay

 **LESSON ONE**

 Intended learning

✦ To discuss the effect of calligrams in poetry.
✦ To invent own calligrams.

 Starting point: Whole class

✦ Share an enlarged version of the poem 'The Night-Time Monster' (page 57) with the children. What do they notice that is different about this poem compared with other poems they have read? Explain that when the formation of the letters or the type of font used in a poem reflect the meaning of the poem, it is called a calligram. Refer them to the words 'hairy' and 'scary' for example. Find all the other words in the poem.
✦ Ask the children whether they think these visual effects enhance or detract from the meaning. Ask them to explain their ideas, referring to the poem.
✦ Ask them if they think some words might be more difficult to write in this way. Find such words in the poem, for example: 'and','the' and 'ever'. What kinds of words do the children think would be the easiest to write in this way? Are they describing words? Remind them of the terms 'noun', 'verb' and 'adjective'. Which words in the

poem are nouns? Write them on the board. Repeat for adjectives and verbs.
✦ What other adjectives could they use to describe a monster? Add these to the list. Challenge the children to choose one of these words and spend a short time writing it to look like its meaning. Model some of your own ideas first.
✦ If time permits, repeat for verbs and nouns. For nouns you could ask the children to write other nouns that might be found in a bedroom or 'night-time' nouns.

 Group activities

✦ One group could be given three boxes with cards inside on which verbs, nouns and adjectives have been written. They pick one word from each box and write the words to look like their meaning, then use them to complete a given poem. For example:
Behind the _____ (noun) a magic rabbit lives,
To everyone a spell he gives,
His _____ (adjective) ears swish and sway,
As he does his magic and _____ (verb) away.
✦ Another group could select a short poem from an anthology that is suitable to turn into a calligram. They need to decide which words to write to look like their meaning.
✦ Another group could write their own calligram by carefully selecting the most appropriate words to describe the subject they are writing about.

 Plenary session

Bring the whole class together again when the children have completed their poems. Ask someone from each group to explain what they had to do. Share some of the poems and how the words were made to look like their meaning. Can others think of different ways to represent some of these words? Which is the most effective? Why? Encourage the children to find other calligrams in anthologies over the coming weeks.

 **LESSON TWO**

Intended learning

✦ To read and share a range of shape poems.
✦ To select appropriate words and style of presentation in writing own shape poem.

Starting point: Whole class

✦ Remind the children about the poem explored in Lesson One. Tell them that sometimes a whole poem can be written in the shape of what it is about. Draw some shapes on the board, such as a wavy line to represent water, a spiral and a rectangle. Ask the children to tell you what the poem might be about if the words in the poem were written inside or along the lines of these shapes. How many different possibilities are there?

✦ Share the poems 'Balloon', 'The Snail', 'Oh To Be a Hexagon' and 'Mouse' on page 57. Ask the children to tell you how each poem reflects the subject. How effective do they think the poems look? Why has the poet presented them in this way? Have they read other shape poems? Which poem do they like best? Why?

✦ Ask the children how they think a poet might go about planning a shape poem. What might come first – the shape or the words? Say that now they are going to write one together.

✦ On the board, draw an outline of a simple shape, such as a kite, the sun or raindrops. Brainstorm some sentences for the poem. How might it begin? Model how to use a thesaurus to find the most suitable words. Agree the lines of the poem. It need only be a simple rhyming couplet, for example:
High in the sky flies my beautiful kite,
Oh how I love such a wonderful sight!

✦ Next draw a larger outline of the chosen shape and fit the words inside or along the outside lines. Explain that the guidelines (the drawing of the shape) can then be deleted in the final version so that the words themselves form the shape of the poem.

✦ Using the differentiated activity sheets

Activity sheet 1

This activity provides a lot of support. It requires the children to select the most appropriate words to complete one poem and then arrange some given words to make another poem.

Activity sheet 2

This activity requires the children to complete two shape poems. In the first poem they are asked to complete two lines of the second verse, following a given pattern. In the second poem, they are given the first line and then have to complete the rest themselves.

Activity sheet 3

This activity is for more able children as it requires them to not only complete a poem but to improve it by using a thesaurus to find better words. They are also required to write a complete poem without support.

 Plenary session

Bring the whole class together again when the children have completed their poems. Ask someone from each group to explain what they had to do. Share some of the poems. How many different poems can be created from the same stimulus? How many different ways could the words in the garden wall poem be arranged and still make sense? Discuss how helpful/restrictive it was to have a subject, shape and poem structure provided. Do the children think the activity has given them confidence to try some shape poems of their own now?

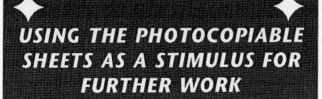

Shape poems

USING THE PHOTOCOPIABLE SHEETS AS A STIMULUS FOR FURTHER WORK

✦ Challenge the children using Activity sheet 1 to make their own 'wall' poems. Ask them to make up a rhyming couplet and then write each word inside a 'brick'. They could ask a partner to re-arrange the 'bricks' to make a poem.

✦ Encourage the children to write their own shape poems, perhaps relating to the class topic. Make them into a class book.

✦ Ask the children to use the same shapes/subjects as on their sheets (star, wall, spider, fork, tree, sea) but make up their own lines for the poems.

✦ Ask the children to write other poems on the same theme, for example poems about the night sky, poems about plants and poems about mini-beasts.

✦ Encourage the children to look through anthologies and find other poems about spiders, trees, stars, food and the sea. Make a collection of them. Ask the children to select a favourite one. Can they turn it into a shape poem, using the same words?

✦ Improve the poems written by using a thesaurus as on Activity sheet 3. The children could work in pairs to try and improve each other's poems.

✦ Turn the poems into large mobiles and hang them from the ceiling in the school library for others to share.

✦ Ask the children to use their poem as part of an advertising campaign and make a poster or jingle. For example, advertising a particular brand of spaghetti or a conservation programme to protect spiders.

OTHER IDEAS FOR USING SHAPE POEMS

✦ Encourage the children to search for shape poems in class/library anthologies. How many can they find? Compare layout/design features – how effective are they?

✦ Make displays on particular subjects more effective by asking the children to find poems on the topic (or write their own) and then turn them into shape poems. For example, an autumn display could have a large tree poem with each line on a branch and other poems could be written inside leaves, falling from the tree.

✦ Develop the idea of shape poems further by considering the emotional side of the poem, rather than the subject. For example, sad poems could be written in the shape of tears or funny poems in the shape of a smile.

✦ Ask the children to make up poems that can be turned into 'textured' calligrams. For example, writing poems about a cat might have the word 'furry' covered in fur material, the word 'tongue' done in sandpaper and 'whisker' done in string.

✦ Perform calligrams by asking the children to make the words sound like their meaning.

16

Using Poetry
KS2: Y3–4/P4–5

✦ Shape poems ✦

✦ Choose the most suitable words from those given to complete this shape poem.

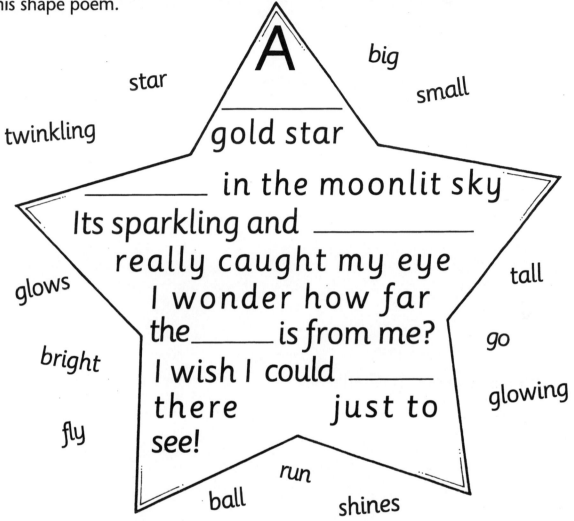

A

star

big

small

twinkling

_____ gold star

_____ in the moonlit sky

Its sparkling and _____

really caught my eye

I wonder how far

the _____ is from me?

I wish I could _____

there   just to

see!

glows

tall

bright

go

glowing

fly

run

ball

shines

✦ Now cut out these words. Use them as 'bricks' to make a shape poem about a garden wall.

wall	hides	tall	garden	it
but	my	things	not	all
is	creepy	very	and	spiders

Developing
literacy
Skills

Photocopiable
© Hopscotch Educational Publishing

✦ Shape poems ✦

✦ Complete this poem about a spider. Use a dictionary to help you.

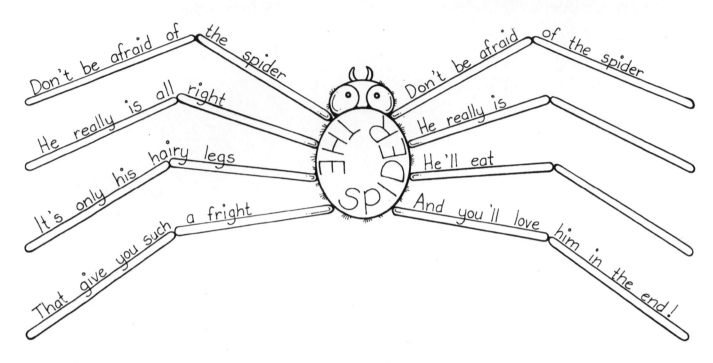

Don't be afraid of the spider
He really is all right
It's only his hairy legs
That give you such a fright

Don't be afraid of the spider
He really is
He'll eat
And you'll love him in the end!

THE RED SPIDER

✦ Finish this poem about spaghetti.

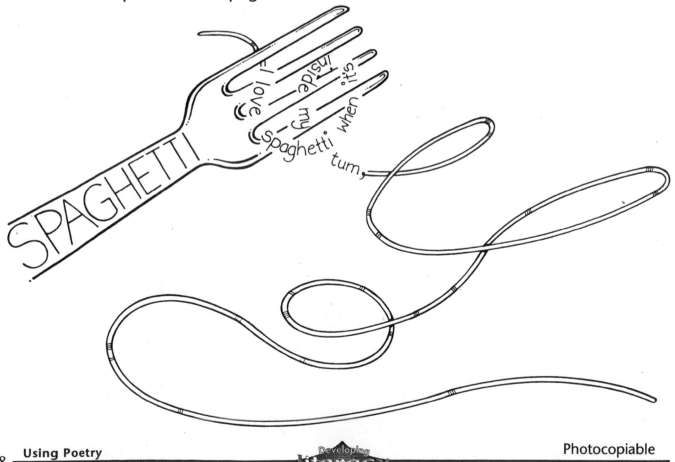

SPAGHETTI

I love
it when it's inside
my spaghetti tum,

Developing
literacy
skills

Photocopiable

✦ Shape poems ✦

✦ Complete this poem by writing the missing lines. Then improve the poem by replacing the circled words with more interesting ones. Use a thesaurus to help you.

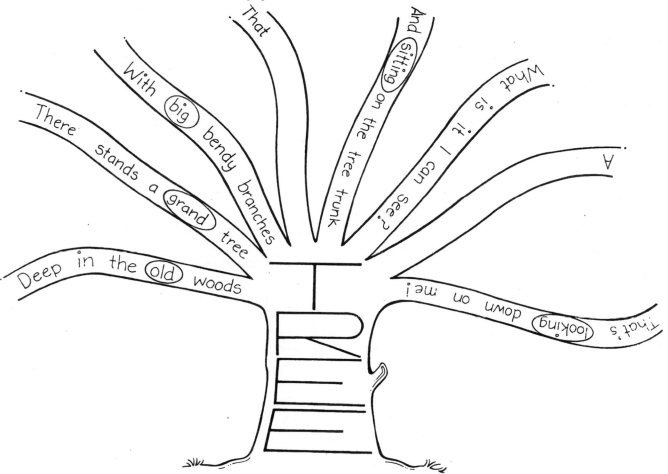

There stands a (grand) tree
With (big) bendy branches
That
And (sitting) on the tree trunk
What is it I can see?
A
That's (looking) down on me!
Deep in the (old) woods

✦ Now use this shape to write your own poem about the sea. Use a dictionary to help you.

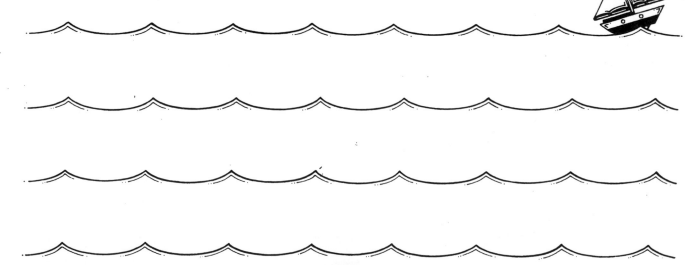

◆ Overall aims

- ✦ To use poems from different cultures to widen children's understanding and experiences.
- ✦ To relate experiences from different cultures to own.
- ✦ To choose and prepare poems for performance.
- ✦ To recognise and generate compound words.

◆ Featured poems (page 58)

Hurricane by Dionne Brand
Roots Man by Grace Walker Gordon
Childhood Tracks by James Berry

◆ LESSON ONE ◆

◆ Intended learning

- ✦ To use poems from different cultures to widen children's understanding and experiences.
- ✦ To choose and prepare a poem for performance.

◆ Starting point: Whole class

- ✦ You may need two lessons to carry out these activities.
- ✦ Tell the children that they are going to read some poems from Jamaica. Use a map to locate Jamaica. Ask the children to tell you anything they know about this country. Show them pictures from books or travel brochures to build up an impression of the landscape and way of life.
- ✦ Ask them to tell you what they think would be different about living in Jamaica compared with where they live. What things might be the same?
- ✦ Share the poem 'Roots Man' (page 58). Ask the children to tell you what they think the poem is trying to tell us. Discuss the meaning of 'roots' in the poem and how the word is used to describe digging up the roots of a crop as well as the 'roots' of past ancestry. Explain how slaves were brought over from Africa to work on big plantations in Jamaica and that is why the man questions where he really comes from.

Ask the children about their family 'roots'. Do any of their parents or grandparents come from other countries?

- ✦ Discuss the use of dialect in the poem. Does this help the poem? How?
- ✦ Is there a rhythm to the poem? Is this intentional? Does it relate to the action of digging the ground?
- ✦ Next, share the poem 'Hurricane' (page 58). How does the language and pace differ from the first poem? Which parts of the poem could be set in this country? Which line tells us it's not here?
- ✦ Explain that the children will have time to explore the poems further by preparing a performance to the rest of the class.

◆ Group activities

- ✦ Divide the children into groups and ask them to carry out the following tasks:
  a) select either 'Hurricane' or 'Roots Man';
  b) decide how to perform the poem – that is, as a whole group together or with individuals taking particular roles;
  c) agree the appropriate expression, volume, tone and use of voice when performing;
  d) decide on the actions and any musical accompaniment needed to support the performance;
  e) rehearse and improve the performance.

◆ Plenary session

Share the finished productions. After each one discuss any problems the children had and how they solved them. Ask others to say what was good about the performance and what could be improved. How well did the children work together? Was this obvious from the finished performance? Did any of the groups manage to create an atmosphere or feeling for Jamaican life? How? If the children were to do this again what things would they improve? Why?

Poems from different cultures

◆ Intended learning

◆ To use poems from different cultures to widen children's understanding and experiences.
◆ To relate experiences from different cultures to own.
◆ To explore words relating to different cultures.
◆ To recognise and generate compound words.

◆ Starting point: Whole class

◆ Remind the children about the poems featured in Lesson One. Tell them that they are going to share another Jamaican poem called 'Childhood Tracks'.
◆ Read the poem and discuss any unfamiliar words. Write them on the board. If possible, have some pictures of a coconut tree, calabash gourd and mango so the children can see what they look like.
◆ Ask the children to tell you the things mentioned in the poem that are different to life in this country, such as the types of food. Notice especially that it is Christmas time and yet the weather is hot! What differences might this make to the celebrations?
◆ Consider those things mentioned in the poem that could also be part of life in this country. How many of the foods mentioned can we buy here? Have any of children eaten coconut, fresh pineapple or mango?
◆ Write the following words on the board: snowball, coconut, pineapples and palmtrees. What do the children notice about all of these words? You might want to point out that in the poem 'palmtrees' is all one word, although it can be spelled as two words. Discuss the meaning of 'compound words' and break each of the words into the separate word parts. What other compound words do the children know? Write a list on the board.
◆ Ask the children to find other compound words in the poem. Add these to the list. Explain that identifying the separate words in a 'compound word' can help us to remember how to spell it. Point out that the title of the poem also contains a compound word. Can the children suggest why the poem has this title?

◆ Tell the children that they will find out about some more words relating to Jamaica by carrying out the next activity.

◆ Using the differentiated activity sheets

Activity sheet 1

This activity provides strong support. The children have to match word parts to make one word. They then use a dictionary to find compound words that begin with a given word part.

Activity sheet 2

This activity is more challenging. The children have to find words of their own and then find compound words that begin and end with given word parts.

Activity sheet 3

This activity requires more independence. The children may need to use the index pages of reference books on native plants and animals in order to find animal and plant names.

◆ Plenary session

Share the names of food, animals, plants and place names of Jamaica. Share meanings of the more difficult word parts such as 'Cam' in Cambridge, 'damsel' in damselfish and 'coco' in coconut. Share the compound words for our country. How many were found? Discuss the task of finding other compound words. Is it more difficult to find words that begin with a particular word part or those that end with one? Ask the children to look up some word meanings from the lists, such as 'en' in entail, 're' in retail and 'cur' in curtail. Encourage the children to look out for other compound words in the coming days and weeks.

Using Poetry
KS2: Y3–4/P4–5

Developing
literacy
Skills

© Hopscotch Educational Publishing   21

Poems from different cultures

◆ USING THE PHOTOCOPIABLE SHEETS AS A STIMULUS FOR FURTHER WORK ◆

◆ Ask the children using Activity sheet 1 to find out about the Jamaican foods. If possible, bring some of them into class so they can see and taste them first-hand. Compare these foods with food grown and eaten in our country.

◆ Ask the children using Activity sheet 2 to find the Jamaican and UK places on a map. Use travel brochures and reference books to find out information about these places.

◆ Ask the children using Activity sheet 3 to find out information about the Jamaican and UK plants and animals. They can compare them to find the differences and similarities between them.

◆ Make a class wall display or book of compound words, beginning with those on the activity sheets. Add to the list over time. Find out the meanings of the word parts. Make word families using the same beginning or ending word parts.

◆ Have fun inventing compound words of your own. For example: a new kind of animal – a furball, a new type of sport – highsliding.

◆ Use the words about Jamaica to write poems about Jamaican food, animals, plants or places.

◆ Make up pictures of compound words for others to guess the word, for example:

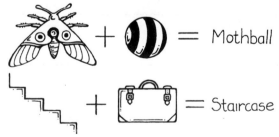

◆ OTHER IDEAS FOR USING POEMS FROM DIFFERENT CULTURES ◆

◆ Make an anthology of poems from around the world. Discuss the differences in format, language, issues/concerns and subject matter between the different countries.

◆ Use poems to introduce language from other countries. Make simple glossaries for the poems so others can understand the meanings of the words used.

◆ Invite local people from different cultural backgrounds to share their favourite poems. Use the time to explore differences and similarities between different cultures.

◆ Dramatise poems for presentation to others. Obtain relevant artefacts to use as props. Make suitable costumes and sound effects/music.

◆ Use poems that raise issues about cultural concerns, such as racism, to introduce some work on the issue.

◆ Write character studies of the person who wrote the poem. Invent where he/she may have lived, what they might look like, clothes they wear and so on by carrying out research on the country the poem originates from.

◆ Ask the children to select suitable poems for a particular purpose, such as poems about growing up in India, poems about animals in Africa, poems about food from Asia. Make class anthologies.

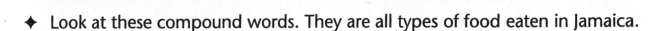

◆ Compound words ◆

◆ Look at these compound words. They are all types of food eaten in Jamaica.

pawpaw   jackfruit   breadfruit   coconut

pineapple   mango   saltfish

◆ Match the words to make compound words of foods eaten in our country.
   One has been done for you.

| straw |
| pan |
| short |
| mush |
| white |
| meat |
| had |
| black |

| currants |
| bait |
| dock |
| cakes |
| rooms |
| berries |
| bread |
| balls |

◆ Use a dictionary to find other compound words that begin with the words
   below. They do not have to be foods. Write as many as you can find.

bread _____

jack _____

man _____

salt _____

black _____

Developing Literacy Skills   © Hopscotch Educational Publishing

✦ Compound words ✦

✦ Look at these compound words. They are all names of places in Jamaica.

   Kingston   Firefly   Cambridge   Mountainside

      Freetown   Portmore   Seaforth   Highgate

✦ Use an atlas to find out names of places in our country that are also
   compound words. Write a list of them here.

   _____

   _____

   _____

   _____

   _____

✦ Use a dictionary to find compound words that begin or end with these
   word parts. The first one has been done for you.

Firefly	Whitehouse	Portmore
fire... – fireplace	white... –	port... –
...fly – butterfly	...house –	...more –
Freetown	Highgate	Cambridge
free... –	high... –	cam... –
...town –	...gate –	...bridge –
Blackburn	Fishguard	Ripon
black... –	fish... –	rip... –
...burn –	...guard –	...on –

Developing
Literacy
Skills

✦ Compound words ✦

✦ Look at these compound words. They are all animals and plants found in Jamaica.

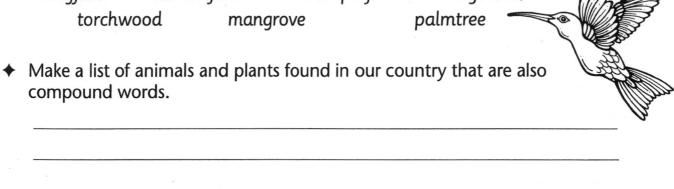

hummingbird   thundersnake   swallowtail butterfly

kingfish   damselfish   trumpetfish   logwood

torchwood   mangrove   palmtree

✦ Make a list of animals and plants found in our country that are also compound words.

_____

_____

_____

✦ Using some of the words in both lists above, find other compound words that either begin or end with the same word parts. The words do not have to be animals and plants. For example:

tail – tailback, tailgate, tailor, tailorbird, tailpiece, tailpipe, tailplane, tailspin, tailwind

bobtail, wagtail, entail, retail, dovetail, curtail

_____

_____

_____

_____

_____

_____

_____

_____

Humorous poems

 ## Overall aims

✦ To compare forms and types of humour in poems.
✦ To select, prepare and read aloud poetry that entertains.
✦ To write poetry that uses sound to create effects.
✦ To give opinions about poems and justify preferences.
✦ To explore verbs, alliteration and onomatopoeia.

 ## Featured poems (page 59)

The London Bus Conductor's Prayer – Anon
Well, Hardly Ever – Anon
The Loch Ness Monster's Song by Edwin Morgan
Granny by Spike Milligan
Limerick – Anon
Mary, Mary by Max Fatchen
The Optimist – Anon

 ## ◆ LESSON ONE ◆

 ## Intended learning

✦ To compare different forms and types of humour in poems.
✦ To give opinions about poems and justify preferences.
✦ To select, prepare and read aloud poetry that entertains.

 ## Starting point: Whole class

✦ Tell the children that they are going to look at a particular type of poem. These are seven short poems, which they may find funny.
✦ Read all the poems on page 59 while the children follow the text. Ask for a show of hands as to their favourite one. Ask them to say briefly why they like the poem and why they think it is funny.
✦ Read through each poem again. Ask the children to say what is or could be funny about each one.

Explain that poems 1 and 6 have changed the words of a well-known prayer and nursery rhyme; poem 5 is a limerick; poem 3 uses made-up words to sound like their meaning (onomatopoeia); poem 2 uses a play on words; poem 4 tells a funny story and poem 7 is like a joke.
✦ Explain that different people find different things funny and therefore not everyone will like all the poems on the page or find all of them funny.
✦ Ask them to tell you about other types of poems they have read which they found funny. Share a humorous poem which is your personal favourite and explain why you find it amusing.

 ## Group activities

✦ Ask the children to use poetry anthologies to complete the following activities:
– Find an amusing poem and write a paragraph explaining why they like it so much and what they find funny about it.
– Find a poem like those on page 59.
– Find a poem for a specific purpose, such as poems to: cheer up someone who is ill, cheer up a grumpy dad or make the teacher smile!
✦ Ask the children to consider how to present the chosen poem. Will the whole group say the poem or will individuals have separate roles? They should think about the right tone of voice to use; how to read the poem so that they take note of the punctuation used, the type of expressions and/or actions to use as well as ways of making their audience sit up and listen!

 ## Plenary session

Bring the whole class together to share each group's poem. Ask each group to justify their choice of poem. Do others share their opinion? Discuss how the poems were read – could the performances be improved in some way?

Make a display or book of the poems, together with the children's writing about why they chose the poem and why they think it is funny.

Humorous poems

 LESSON TWO

✦ Intended learning

✦ To explore verbs, alliteration and onomatopoeia.
✦ To write poems that use sound to create effects.

✦ Starting point: Whole class

✦ Remind the children about the work carried out using humorous poems in Lesson One. Tell them that they are going to try writing their own humorous poem. Explain that this will be made easier because they will be using a particular pattern.
✦ Enlarge and share the following poem:

Farmyard Cacophony
Ducks quacking
Dogs barking
Cows mooing
Tractor chugging
Horses neighing
Farmer humming
Geese hissing
Wind whistling
Birds singing
Chickens clucking

✦ Talk about the pattern used in the poem – how each thing on the farm has a verb to describe the noise it makes and how each verb ends in '-ing'. Point out that the farm noises have also been emphasised by the use of sound effects created by onomatopoeic words and alliteration.
✦ Now show the children this poem:

Ducks neighing
Dogs mooing
Cows singing
Tractor clucking
Horses quacking
Farmer hissing
Geese barking
Wind chugging
Birds humming
Chickens whistling

✦ Ask what has happened to the verbs in the second poem (they have been swapped around to make humorous associations). Explain that by moving the words around and re-arranging them, we can end up with a humorous poem.
✦ Tell them that they will now have the opportunity to create their own poem in the same way.

✦ Using the differentiated activity sheets

The children could write their own humorous verb poems after completing the activity sheets.

Activity sheet 1

This is aimed at those children who need more support. They are required to re-arrange given verbs to create their poem.

Activity sheet 2

This is for more independent workers who are capable of completing the poem using given verbs or ones of their own choice.

Activity sheet 3

This is for more able children. It requires them to use a dictionary and thesaurus to find synonyms for given verbs and then re-arrange the verbs to make a funny poem.

✦ Plenary session

Bring the whole class together when they have completed the activities. Read the original poem for each group and then ask some children from the group to read out their humorous version. Explore different possibilities for making even funnier endings. Would it be possible to make the whole poem alliterative? Check that the spellings of the verbs used are correct and use this time to reinforce spelling rules for adding '-ing'.

Using Poetry
KS2: Y3–4/P4–5

Developing
literacy
Skills

© Hopscotch Educational Publishing 27

USING THE PHOTOCOPIABLE SHEETS AS A STIMULUS FOR FURTHER WORK

✦ Ask half the class to write one noun from their activity sheet and half the class to write a verb onto a piece of paper. Put the words into two containers and ask children to select one of each to make a class poem or challenge them to make up a funny sentence including the two words.

✦ Use the activities to extend work on verbs. Build up word families of similar verbs; find words which do not conform to spelling rules (such as not dropping 'e' before adding 'ing' – dye, dyeing); find synonyms and antonyms of commonly-used verbs.

✦ Explore adjectives by adding them to the poems, for example: 'baby crying' becomes *'little baby crying'*.

✦ Challenge the children to write their own ABC verb poem as in Activity sheet 3 or extend the activity to write alliterations, for example: 'cars careering continually'.

✦ Make a class book of the funny poems and ask the children to draw the funniest lines, such as a vacuum crying, to illustrate the book.

✦ Challenge the children to draw verbs to look like their meaning, for example:

OTHER IDEAS FOR USING HUMOROUS POEMS

✦ Make up humorous rhymes for autograph books, such as:

> *Roses are red*
> *Violets are blue*
> *I am the greatest*
> *And so are you!*

✦ Challenge the children to make up verses using a play on letters and symbols, for example:

11 was a race horse 22 was 12 1111 race 22112	I'm in a 10der mood today & feel poetic, 2 4 fun I'll just – off a line & send it off 2 U

✦ Write humorous question-and-answer poems that use homonyms, for example:

> *Where can the carpenter find ten nails?*
> *On the end of his fingers.*
> *Where can you sit to find shade on a hot day?*
> *Under the palms of your hand.*

✦ Re-write nursery rhymes to make them humorous. Inspire the children by reading Roald Dahl's *Revolting Rhymes*.

✦ The children could read and then write their own nonsense poems:

> *A peanut sat on the railroad track,*
> *His heart was all a-flutter.*
> *Along came a train –*
> *Toot-toot! – peanut butter!*

✦ Funny noises! ✦

✦ Cut out the words in this poem. Re-arrange them to make a new funny poem. Glue the words onto another sheet of paper. Draw pictures to go with your poem.

Home Sweet Home?

baby	crying
dishwasher	whirring
television	blaring
dog	barking
vacuum	humming
telephone	ringing
tap	dripping
children	yelling
dad	snoring
kittens	purring
door	banging
frying pan	sizzling

Developing literacy skills

◆ Funny noises! ◆

◆ Complete this poem by writing suitable verbs at the end of each line. You can use some of the verbs in the box or use a dictionary to find your own.

The Seaside

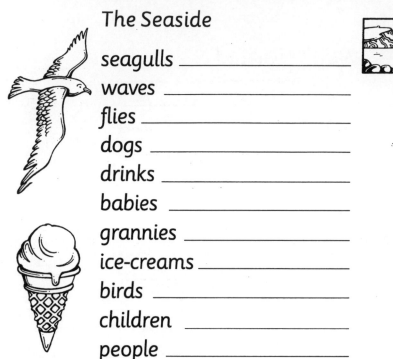

seagulls _____

waves _____

flies _____

dogs _____

drinks _____

babies _____

grannies _____

ice-creams _____

birds _____

children _____

people _____

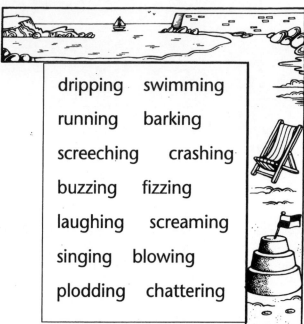

dripping	swimming
running	barking
screeching	crashing
buzzing	fizzing
laughing	screaming
singing	blowing
plodding	chattering

◆ Now re-arrange the verbs to make a funny poem about the seaside.

For example, instead of

seagulls screeching
and
waves crashing

You might write:

seagulls laughing
and
waves barking

◆ Use the back of this sheet to make up a funny verb poem of your own!

The Seaside

seagulls _____

waves _____

flies _____

dogs _____

drinks _____

babies _____

grannies _____

ice-creams _____

birds _____

children _____

people _____

Developing
Literacy
Skills

✦ Funny noises! ✦

✦ Read this poem about noises. Then use a dictionary and a thesaurus to find a synonym for each verb. The first one has been done for you.

Noisy ABC!

cars accelerating	cars <u>speeding</u>
bulls bellowing	bulls _____
children chortling	children _____
people dancing	people _____
champagne effervescing	champagne _____
flags flapping	flags _____
teeth gnawing	teeth _____
wolf howling	wolf _____
fire igniting	fire _____
keys jangling	keys _____
knees knocking	knees _____
baby laughing	baby _____
ladies murmuring	ladies _____
boys nattering	boys _____
mud oozing	mud _____
ears popping	ears _____
ducks quacking	ducks _____
lions roaring	lions _____
pigs squealing	pigs _____
fingers tapping	fingers _____
men uttering	men _____
violin vibrating	violin _____
siren wailing	siren _____
bomb eXploding	bomb _____
dogs yapping	dogs _____
laser zapping	laser _____

✦ Now re-arrange the verbs on the end of each line to make a funny poem about noises. Write your new poem on the back of this sheet.

Overall aims

✦ To explore word puzzles such as riddles, puns and word games.
✦ To invent own riddles and puzzles.
✦ To explore homophones.

 Featured poems (page 60)

Collection of riddles – Anon
No Wonder I Can't Spell! by Frances Mackay

 **LESSON ONE**

 Intended learning

✦ To explore different kinds of riddles.
✦ To write own riddles.

 Starting point: Whole class

✦ Tell the children that they are going to look at riddles today. Ask them to tell you what they know about riddles. Have they read any riddles in a class or school anthology? Do they know of any stories with riddles in them (such as *The Hobbit*)?
✦ Tell them that there are several different kinds of riddles. Demonstrate this in shared reading by using the riddles on page 60. Numbers 1 and 2 are the type which spell out an answer. Each line gives a clue to the letters in the word. The words used in each line are associated with each other. These riddles usually use rhyming couplets. Numbers 3 and 4 are much simpler rhyming couplets which describe the object in clue form. Numbers 5 and 6 are question riddles that require a responding answer. Numbers 7 and 8 describe the object in more detail. Number 8, especially, uses very poetic and descriptive language and tries not to give away the answer too easily. The answers are: 1. fish 2. bird 3. smoke 4. chimney 5. newspaper 6. Because it saw the salad dressing 7. robin 8. egg.

✦ Ask the children to tell you the similarities and differences between the types of riddles represented on the page. Which types of riddles have they come across before? Which type do they find the most difficult? Why? What do they notice about the endings of the lines? Discuss the fact that many riddles use rhyme. Find the words which rhyme in these riddles.
✦ Model writing a riddle of the type represented by 1 and 2 by asking the class to come up with a word and then inventing the clues together.

 Group activities

✦ Working in pairs or small groups, challenge the children to write their own riddles modelled on examples 1, 2, 3, 4, 7 and 8. If possible, make a rhyming dictionary available or a word bank of rhyming words.
✦ Ask the children to collect and sort into categories (such as those on page 60) other examples of riddles from class poetry anthologies. Use them to begin a class collection.

 Plenary session

Bring the whole class together again when the children have completed the activities. Ask several children to read out their riddles to the others. Can they work out the answers? Discuss the problems encountered in doing the tasks. How were these overcome? Share some of the riddles collected from other sources. How many of each kind were found? Which type of riddle appears to be the most common in the classroom anthologies?

◆ LESSON TWO ◆

◆ Intended learning

◆ To explore word puzzles such as puns and word games.
◆ To discuss the meaning of homophones and to explore different meanings of words.

◆ Starting point: Whole class

◆ Photocopy or enlarge the poem 'No Wonder I Can't Spell!' (page 60) and share it with the children. Discuss the problem mentioned in the poem. Do the children also think that it is annoying to have words that sound the same but are spelled differently and have a different meaning? Tell them that these words are called 'homophones'.
◆ Ask them to tell you how to spell the homophones of other words in the poem – such as 'not', 'which', 'I', 'so', 'sure', 'you', 'there', 'see', 'use' (ewes), 'done' (dun), 'we' and 'would'. Use these words and the given homophones in the poem to make a class list of homophones. Tell the children that they will be adding to this list as part of their work in this lesson.
◆ Explain that sometimes people have fun using homophones by deliberately using a different meaning of a word to make a funny remark. Say that these are called 'puns'. Give the children some examples and ask them to explain the humour in each one. For example:
*The most important part of a horse is the **main** part.*
*The strongest type of shell-fish is a **mussel**.*
*The only thing going **cheap** at Christmas is the robin.*
*She's just **dying** to change her hair colour.*
◆ Ask the children if they know of any other puns. Invite them to do some homework by asking people at home for puns that they can share with the class at another time. In the meantime, explain that they are going to find out about some more homophones by carrying out a word puzzle activity.

◆ Using the differentiated activity sheets

All three sheets require the children to do the same task. The sheets are graded, however, with the easiest words on Activity sheet 1 and the most difficult on Activity sheet 3. When the activity sheets have been completed, challenge the children in all three groups to use the homophones from their activity sheets to make up some puns of their own.

Activity sheet 1

This activity is for less able readers. In guided reading, the teacher can help the children to read the words and definitions.

Activity sheet 2

This activity is for more independent workers. Some of the clues are more cryptic.

Activity sheet 3

This activity is for more able children. They may need to use a dictionary to check the meaning of the more obscure words.

◆ Plenary session

Bring the whole class together again when the children have completed the sheets. Check the answers with each group. How many other homophones did the children write down? Add these to the list started at the beginning of the lesson. Invite the children to add to this list over the coming weeks. Ask them if they invented any puns using the words. Share their ideas or make up some together.

Using Poetry
KS2: Y3–4/P4–5

Developing
literacy
Skills

© Hopscotch Educational Publishing

33

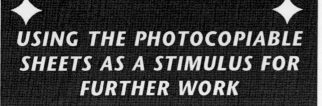

Word puzzles

◆ USING THE PHOTOCOPIABLE SHEETS AS A STIMULUS FOR FURTHER WORK ◆

◆ Have fun by asking the children to draw humorous homophones, such as a bare bear, a dear deer, a fir tree with fur, a buoy like a boy, a barque barking and so on.

◆ Make a class dictionary of homophones with drawings and definitions of the words. Use it as a resource bank for writing.

◆ Challenge the children to make up a poem using homophones.

◆ Ask the children to write their own clues for the homophones they collected, then try them out on others.

◆ Make word searches where the children have to find the homophones for the words listed.

◆ Make up crossword puzzles with homophone answers and puns as clues.

◆ Make a display of 'punny' things containing drawings and sentences of puns.

◆ OTHER IDEAS FOR USING WORD PUZZLES ◆

◆ Investigate compound words. Make up puzzles where the children have to match two words to make one word.

◆ Read and share acrostic poems where the first letter of each line makes a word. Challenge the children to write their own acrostics.

◆ Investigate palindromes – words and phrases that can be read backwards and forwards, for example:
mum, madam, level, refer, radar, kayak, noon, dad, wet stew, was it a cat I saw?
Can the children find/make up some more?

◆ Challenge the children to explore anagrams where they have to re-arrange the letters in a word to make new words, for example:
    team – mate, meat, tame
All the letters in the original word must be used to make each new word.

◆ Read and write some 'knock-knock' jokes, especially those that rely on a play on words.

◆ Invent words which describe something without using its proper name (kennings). For example:
    cat = mouse-chaser
    television = goggle-box
Make up poems using the kennings.

◆ Explore spoonerisms, for example:
    Figs on a palm = pigs on a farm
    A boiled sprat = a spoiled brat
Challenge the children to make up their own.
Have fun illustrating them!

34
© Hopscotch Educational Publishing

Developing
Literacy
Skills

Using Poetry
KS2: Y3–4/P4–5

Activity 1   Name _____

✦ Homophones ✦

✦ Read the clues below and draw a line from the clue to the correct word in the lists.

blue
fir
write
rode
sun
flu
so
pore
been
sail
deer
you
hair
bye
bee
bare

Clues:
It's not a rabbit!
A female sheep
The colour of the sky
A green vegetable
A large furry mammal
It gives our Earth light
Something expensive
The opposite to left
An insect that makes honey
Another word for farewell
A very bad cold
Type of tree used at Christmas
Joining fabric together with thread
Attached to the mast on a yacht
Not rich
Another name for a street

blew
fur
right
road
son
flew
sew
poor
bean
sale
dear
ewe
hare
buy
be
bear

✦ How many other homophones do you know? Write them on the back of this sheet. Use a dictionary to help you look for words.

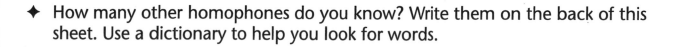

✦ Homophones ✦

✦ Read the clues below and draw a line from the clue to the correct word in the lists.

	Clues:	
heir	A computer's teeth!	air
allowed	Nothing to do	aloud
beach	Another name for perfume	beech
byte	You need one to play tennis	bite
bored	The past tense of 'throw'	board
boy	Male child living in the sea!	buoy
weather	Opposite to 'mend'	whether
plaice	Type of tree	place
fought	Person who inherits property	fort
dyeing	Good with chips	dying
through	Something people always talk about!	threw
fare	Permitted	fair
cheap	Not expensive	cheep
scent	Could be a castle	sent
caught	Bus charge	court
break	Not going to live	brake

✦ How many other homophones do you know? Write them on the back of this sheet. Use a dictionary to help you look for words.

Developing
literacy
Skills

✦ Homophones ✦

✦ Read the clues below and draw a line from the clue to the correct word in the lists. Use a dictionary to check the meanings of words you do not know.

	Clues:	
stationery	Small glass medicine container	stationary
guerilla	A mock attack	gorilla
phial	To change something	file
practice	A sailing ship	practise
aisle	A landing place for ships	isle
bark	To give up the right to do something	barque
bridle	Not moving	bridal
sealing	A secret soldier	ceiling
waive	Not very fine	wave
quay	Used instead of money	key
jam	The top of a room	jamb
faint	Headgear for a horse	feint
cheque	The front of a ship	check
bough	Passage between seats in a church	bow
alter	To do something repeatedly	altar
course	Door post	coarse

✦ How many other homophones do you know? Write them on the back of this sheet. Use a dictionary to help you look for words.

Overall aims

✦ To compare and contrast poems on the same theme.
✦ To discuss personal responses and preferences.
✦ To explore verbs and synonyms.
✦ To write own poem linked to poems read.

 Featured poems (pages 61 and 62)

The Sloojee by Colin West
The Snitterjipe by James Reeves
The Ghoul by Jack Prelutsky
The Boodlespook – Anon

 **LESSON ONE**

 Intended learning

✦ To compare and contrast poems on a similar theme.
✦ To discuss personal responses and preferences.

 Starting point: Whole class

✦ Read each poem, or just two, from pages 61 and 62 and ask the children to write down a few words/sentences to give a brief instant reaction to them. Allow a few minutes for the children to share their responses with a partner.
✦ Very briefly, ask for a show-of-hands in response to questions such as: *who likes this poem a lot/little/ not at all? Who finds it funny/scary/very descriptive?* and so on.
✦ Discuss the titles of the poems. Why are most of them strange names? Does the language used in the poem help to build up an image in their minds of what the monster might look like? Ask the children to give an example of such language in the poems.
✦ Tell the children they will now have an opportunity to explore the poems further.

 Group activities

✦ One group could work in pairs. Ask each child to draw a sketch of the Boodlespook, using the text as a reference. Allow only a short time for this – it is not the drawing that is important, but the children's discussion of the poem afterwards. Ask the pairs to share their sketches. How similar are they? Are the descriptions in the poem explicit enough to enable the reader to obtain enough detail of what the monster looks like? Is there anything important missing in the description – is it possible to draw all the monster's body accurately? Ask them to label their drawings using lines from the poem.
✦ Another group could write a paragraph about their favourite poem from the collection. Encourage them to justify their opinions by referring to words/lines used in the poem. Ask them to consider the form of the poem. How important is the layout? Does the poet use rhyme? How effective is this?
✦ A third group could decide which monster they think is the most frightening. Ask them to justify their opinion by referring to the way the poet has described the monster and people's reactions to it. They should compare the poets' treatments of each monster.

 Plenary session

Compare the sketches of the Boodlespook and discuss the effectiveness of the poet's use of language to describe the monster and how this helped/hindered their drawings. Ask someone from the group who has selected a favourite poem to share their responses. Why did they prefer this poem? They should back up their responses with references to the text. Finally, ask someone from the last group to say which monster they would find the most frightening and why. Do others agree? Are monsters always portrayed as being frightening? Do the children enjoy being frightened by such tales? Why?

◆ LESSON TWO ◆

◆ Intended learning

- ✦ To explore the use of powerful verbs.
- ✦ To explore synonyms.
- ✦ To write own poem using verbs linked to poems read.

◆ Starting point: Whole class

- ✦ Re-read 'The Sloojee' by Colin West (page 61). Ask the children to tell you the things listed in the poem that the monster makes people do. Write the words on the board.
- ✦ Remind the children what verbs are and ask them which words in the list are verbs. Underline them. Discuss the appropriateness of the verbs used. Do they accurately describe what a monster might make people do? What other verbs can the children think of to add to the list? What things might they do if they saw a monster?
- ✦ Select some of the verbs, such as 'cry' and 'scream'. Ask the children to tell you other verbs that have the same meaning. How could they find more powerful or more expressive words? Discuss the use of a thesaurus and the term 'synonym'. Find more powerful verbs for some of the listed words. Allow the children an opportunity to look up some words themselves. Remind them that they must make sure the alternative word also has an appropriate/ equivalent meaning.
- ✦ Look again at the poem. Discuss how the poet uses rhyme. Might this have an effect on the verbs he has chosen? Could alternative verbs be used and still fit the pattern and form of the poem? How do the children think a poet decides what is the best word to use?
- ✦ Tell the children that they will now have an opportunity to write their own poem using verbs.

◆ Using the differentiated activity sheets

Activity sheet 1

This activity is for children who still need practice in using a dictionary to find words. It has the alphabet on the page to support them and a space to draw their own monster. Teachers may find it appropriate to sit with this group to help them use a thesaurus to find more powerful verbs for some of the words selected by the children.

Activity sheet 2

This activity is for more confident users of thesauruses. They are provided with some support for the more difficult words.

Activity sheet 3

This activity is for more able children and uses more difficult verbs. The activity could be extended further by asking the children to find antonyms for the verbs selected.

◆ Plenary session

Bring the whole class together again after the children have completed the poems. Ask several children from each group to read out their poems. Discuss the verbs selected. Are they appropriate? Could more powerful alternatives be used? Discuss the meaning of any words the children are unfamiliar with. Consider making the monster a friendly one by reminding the children that a thesaurus can also be used to find antonyms. Challenge the children to find some antonyms for some of the verbs.

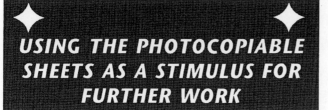

◆ USING THE PHOTOCOPIABLE SHEETS AS A STIMULUS FOR FURTHER WORK ◆

✦ Encourage the children to write their own poems about monsters using powerful and expressive verbs.

✦ Make up a class thesaurus of monster words, beginning with those in the poems and the activity sheets. Use the thesaurus for writing a story about monsters.

✦ Make a wall ABC chart of monster words.

✦ Use the verbs to write alliterative sentences about monsters, for example:
Many mysterious monsters mangled, mutilated, munched, mauled, mistreated, muddied and mugged my magnificent machines.

✦ Use the activity sheets as a starting point for exploring adjectives. Make up ABC poems to describe monsters.

✦ Turn the poems into an ABC story book about monsters with verbs on every page.

✦ Ask the children to use information books to find out about 'real' monsters, such as the Loch Ness Monster or the Abominable Snowman.

✦ Write newspaper reports about monsters or make up television reports to act out.

✦ Challenge the children to dramatise a documentary-style drama about investigating a monster (a 'docu-soap' type television production where the children interview people as well as tell the story).

◆ OTHER IDEAS FOR USING POEMS WITH THE SAME THEME ◆

✦ Make class anthologies of poems on the same theme with a paragraph from each child saying why they selected the poem for the anthology.

✦ Use the poems as a stimulus for the children to write their own poems on the same theme.

✦ Use the poems on pages 61 – 62 to study how different poets have approached the same theme.

✦ Challenge the children to select a poem which they consider best represents the chosen theme. For example, a poem that best illustrates what it's really like to have a good friend, visit the seaside and so on. Ask the children to prepare a short talk to the rest of the class explaining why they have selected the poem. Encourage them to refer to particular words or lines in the poem to illustrate a point they want to make.

✦ Make inviting boxes of poems by covering boxes with images of the chosen theme and putting poems inside. Encourage the children to find more poems themselves to add to the collection.

✦ Make a poet-tree of poets who have written poems on the same theme. Display it in the library as a reference source.

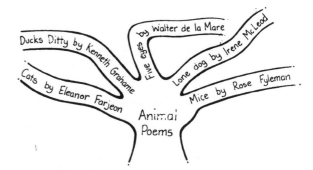

◆ Monster ABC ◆

◆ Complete this ABC poem about a terrible monster by writing
  a suitable verb in each space. Use a dictionary to help you.
  Invent a name for the monster.

The _____ is a horrible creature.

It can:

a __attack__ you,
b _____ you,
c _____ you,
d _drill_ you,
e _____ you,
f _____ you,
g _____ you,
h _____ you,
i _infect_ you,
j _____ you,
k _____ you,
l _____ you,
m _____ you,
n _____ you,
o _offend_ you,
p _____ you,
q _quarter_ you,
r _____ you,
s _____ you,
t _____ you,
u _____ you,
v _vacuum_ you,
w _____ you,
x _eXterminate_ you,
y _____ you, or
z _zap_ you!!!

Draw a picture of your monster here:

✦ Monster ABC ✦

✦ Read this ABC poem about a monster. Then re-write the poem by using a thesaurus to find synonyms for each verb, beginning with the same letter of the alphabet. Some of the verbs have been completed for you. Invent a name for the monster.

The _____ is a horrible creature.

It can:

annoy you,   _____ you,

belt you,   _____ you,

chop you,   _____ you,

dissolve you,   _____ you,

entrap you,   ___entangle___ you,

frizzle you,   ___fry___ you,

grab you,   _____ you,

harm you,   _____ you,

inject you,   _____ you,

jolt you,   _____ you,

knot you,   ___knit___ you,

lap you,   ___lick___ you,

mangle you,   _____ you,

nibble you,   _____ you,

overcome you,   _____ you,

prod you,   _____ you,

quiz you,   ___question___ you,

repel you,   _____ you,

stab you,   _____ you,

trick you,   _____ you,

unsettle you,   ___upset___ you,

vex you,   ___peeVe___ you,

wobble you,   ___waver___ you,

eXtinguish you,   _____ you,

yell at you,   ___yelp at___ you,

or ZAP you!!!

Photocopiable
© Hopscotch Educational Publishing

✦ Monster ABC ✦

✦ Read this ABC poem about a monster. Then re-write the poem by using
a thesaurus to find synonyms for each verb, beginning with the same
letter of the alphabet. Some of the verbs have been completed for you.
Invent a name for the monster.

The _____ is a horrible creature.

It can:

antagonise you,   _____ you,

bewilder you,   _____ you,

chastise you,   _____ you,

dissect you,   _____ you,

eradicate you,   _____ you,

flatten you,   _____ you,

guzzle you,   _____ you,

harass you,   _____ you,

incapacitate you,   _immobilise_____ you,

jostle you,   _____ you,

knuckle you,   _knead_____ you,

lunge at you,   _____ at you,

mutilate you,   _____ you,

neutralise you,   _____ you,

outmanoeuvre you,   _____ you,

pierce you,   _____ you,

quash you,   _____ you,

rebuke you,   _____ you,

startle you,   _____ you,

terrorise you,   _____ you,

uncover you,   _unearth_____ you,

vilify you,   _vituperate_____ you,

wither you,   _____ you,

eXterminate you,   _____ you,

yap at you,   _____ at you,

or ZAP you!!!

Overall aims

✦ To discuss the meaning of 'classic' poetry.
✦ To identify clues which suggest poems are older.
✦ To explore similes.
✦ To write own poem based on those read.

 Featured poems (page 63)

To a Fish of the Brook by John Walcot (1738–1819)
The Fly by Walter de la Mare (1873–1956)
Sweet Suffolk Owl by Thomas Vautor (16th century)
Upon the Snail by John Bunyan (1628–1688)

◆ LESSON ONE ◆

 Intended learning

✦ To discuss the meaning of 'classic' poetry.
✦ To identify clues which suggest poems are older.

◆ **Starting point: Whole class**

✦ Enlarge a copy of 'To a Fish of the Brook' by John Walcott (page 63). Tell the children that they will be reading some classic poems today. Ask them to tell you what they think the word 'classic' means. Refer to a dictionary to add to their ideas. What stories do they know that could be called classics? Do they know any poems that might be called classic?

✦ Tell them that you are going to share with them a poem about a fish. Ask them to think about why this poem might be a classic as you read it through. Make sure that they can see the poem as you read it. What do they think is happening in the poem? What words are used that tell us that the poem may have been written long ago? Underline these words and discuss their meanings. What might be the equivalent modern-day words for each one? Are any of these words sometimes

still used today ('naught', for example)? Read the poem through again, together.

✦ Ask the children to guess how old the poem might be. Why do they say this? Tell them that the poet was born in 1738 and died in 1819. Ask them if they think the subject matter of the poem is just as relevant today. What words are still used today ('angler', 'brook', 'bait')? What words used in the poem have changed their meaning ('wicked')?

✦ Tell the children that they will now have the opportunity to explore some other classic poems in a similar way.

 Group activities

✦ Provide copies of 'The Fly', 'Sweet Suffolk Owl' and 'Upon the Snail' (page 63).

✦ One group could underline the words they think are no longer used today. Ask them to select five to ten of these words and write what they think the modern-day meaning might be.

✦ Another group could substitute modern-day words in one of the poems to re-write it in modern-day language and expressions.

✦ More able children could write a glossary of terms to accompany the poems containing researched or invented meanings for words such as 'dight', 'gare' and 'looking-glass'.

 Plenary session

Do all the children agree that the poems were written long ago? Ask those who were underlining words to share their list. Agree on the meaning for some of these words. (Note that 'dight' means 'dressed'.) What other clues tell us the poems were written long ago (for example, 'feather bed', 'looking-glass')? Ask some children to read their re-written poem. Does it sound as good as the original? Why or why not? What meanings did the group writing the glossary come up with? Are they acceptable/accurate?

Classic Poems

 LESSON TWO

✦ Intended learning

✦ To explore similes.
✦ To write own poem based on those read.

✦ Starting point: Whole class

✦ Tell the children that they are going to explore one of the poems from Lesson One. Share 'The Fly' (page 63). Remind them that this poem was written quite a long time ago and ask them to tell you some of the clues in the poem that tell us this.

✦ What else do they notice about how the poem is written? They might notice the alternate lines rhyming and that the poem uses the words 'like' or 'as' throughout. Explain that lines such as 'A rosebud like a feather bed' and 'The smallest grain of mustard-seed as fierce as coals of fire' are called similes – phrases that use the words 'like' or 'as' to compare something with something else. Tell them that many classic and modern-day poems use similes to help describe things to the reader.

✦ Ask them to find all the similes in the poem. How good are the comparisons? Can a dewdrop be like a mirror? Is mustard as hot as fire? Why has the poet used similes? How has it helped the poem?

✦ Explain that similes are also used in everyday language, both in the past and today, such as: 'as blind as a bat', 'as dry as a bone' and 'as black as coal'. List some others. Which of these do the children think are most descriptive? Why? Would the use of similes help us to understand the meaning of something new to us or help us build up a picture of the object in our mind's eye? Read out the following poem to see if the children can guess what kind of animal it is describing:

> He needs
> A coat like thick brown moss,
> A head like a sculptured rock,
> Claws like metal combs,
> Paws like boxing gloves,
> And a growl like rumbling thunder.

('How To Make a Bear' – Anon)

✦ Explore the idea of similes a little further by asking the children to think up descriptions for things in the school, such as 'The hall is as big as a house', 'The field is like a green sea' or 'The playground is as hard as rock'.

✦ Tell them that they will now have an opportunity to write a poem of their own using similes.

✦ Using the differentiated activity sheets

The children could work in small groups, pairs or individually on these activity sheets. Make available dictionaries, a rhyming dictionary and thesauruses.

Activity sheet 1

This activity is aimed at children who need more support with ideas and vocabulary. The poem uses a simple rhyming couplet pattern.

Activity sheet 2

This activity provides the children with some support but also enables them to introduce ideas of their own.

Activity sheet 3

This activity is for more able children who are capable of writing their own simile poem with minimum support.

✦ Plenary session

Ask several children from each group to read out their poems. How many different ideas could be found for the same poem? Which similes do the children particularly like? Why? Does the use of rhyme help or hinder writing the poem? Does having a pattern/idea to follow help in writing a poem?

Using Poetry
KS2: Y3–4/P4–5

Classic Poems

◆ USING THE PHOTOCOPIABLE SHEETS AS A STIMULUS FOR FURTHER WORK

◆ Make a poetry anthology about friends and family, beginning with the poems on the activity sheets. Find poems in books to add to the collection as well as the children's own poems.

◆ Encourage the children to find other poems that use similes. Build up a collection to compare the effectiveness of the comparisons used in the similes.

◆ Write stories about Fred, Su Lee, Pan, Millie, Uncle Horace and Aunt Maisie.

◆ Make up crossword puzzles with similes as clues.

◆ Ask the children to draw pictures of people. Swap the picture with a partner and ask the partner to write a simile poem about the picture.

◆ Write simile poems about animals for others to guess what the creature is.

◆ Draw funny pictures to illustrate similes, for example 'He was as dry as a bone' and 'The dog was as black as coal'.

◆ OTHER IDEAS FOR USING CLASSIC POEMS

◆ Challenge the children to write a 'classic' poem of their own, mimicking the form and language of poems read.

◆ Omit the last verse of a classic poem and ask the children to write the last verse in the same style.

◆ Encourage the children to collect poems by particular poets to compare style, subject treatment and language used.

◆ Read a classic poem to the children once a week to familiarise them with a wide range of poets and language used.

◆ Ask the children to write a glossary for a poem to help others understand the meaning of the words used.

◆ Act out the poems on page 63 to practise using the archaic expressions and patterns of ryhme.

◆ Compare modern-day poems with classics on the same theme. How do the subject treatment and language used differ?

◆ Ask the children to conduct a survey of their parents/grandparents to find out what their favourite poems are. Are these poems still relevant to children today? Why do some poems endure the passing of time and not others?

◆ Explore patterns of rhyme in poems. Explain terms such as 'rhyming couplet' and 'alternate line rhyme'.

✦ Similes ✦

✦ Read this poem. It contains lots of similes.

I have a friend called Fred
Who has the weirdest head!
He's got sticky-up hair
Like a prickly pear.
He's got big blue eyes
Like buzzing flies.
He's got a long sharp nose
Like a thorny rose.
He's got a great long chin
Like a baked bean tin.
And sticky-out ears
Like jugs of beer!

✦ Now finish the poem below using your own ideas for similes to complete each line. Use the words in the box or a rhyming dictionary to help you.

I have a friend called Su Lee
Who is as _____ as can be!
She's got curly hair
Like _____
She's got deep dark eyes
Like _____
She's got a small round nose
Like _____
She's got a nice smooth chin
Like _____
And cute little ears
Like _____

chair	bear	mare
flare	pear	stair
sky	sty	thigh
pie	fly	tie
hose	bellows	rose
primrose	bin	pin
robin	ruin	deer
tear	pier	sphere

✦ On the back of this sheet, draw a picture of Su Lee.

♦ Similes ♦

✦ Read this poem. It contains lots of similes.

I have a friend called Pan
Who's a very strange looking man.
He's got wild and woolly hair
Like a wild and ferocious bear.
He's got eyes that dart and flick
Like a snake that moves real quick.
He's got a huge and bulbous nose
Like a bud on a garden rose.
He's got a mouth that's big and wide
Like a hole you jump inside.
Yes, he's strange, that's for sure
But he'll be my friend for ever more!

✦ Now complete the poem below using your own ideas for similes to complete each line. Draw a picture of Millie to show what she looks like.

I have a friend called Millie
Who really looks quite silly!
She's got _____
Like _____
She's got _____
Like _____
She's got _____
Like _____
She's got _____
Like _____
Yes, Millie is a sight to see,
But she's as kind as can be!

✦ On the back of this page write another poem about a strange friend!

◆ Similes ◆

✦ Read this poem. It contains lots of similes.

Uncle Horace

My uncle Horace wears shirts like sails on a boat,
Baggy trousers like an elephant's behind
And flowery ties like a botanical garden!
His hair is as black as the darkest night
And his beard is as long as the longest snake!
His eyes glitter and gleam like stars in the sky,
His nose glows like a lighthouse beacon
And his teeth sparkle like glittering gems!
Yes, he's a weird and wonderful sight
But I can't stop loving him, try as I might!

✦ Now look at this picture of Aunt Maisie and write a poem about her. Use similes
to describe what she looks like and what she is wearing.

Using Poetry
KS2: Y3–4/P4–5

Developing
literacy
skills

Photocopiable
© Hopscotch Educational Publishing

49

Overall aims

- To explore patterns of rhyme in poetry and to describe how a poet does or does not use rhyme.
- To recognise simple forms of poetry and their uses.
- To explore the use of syllables in poems.
- To write poems, experimenting with different styles and structures.

 ## Featured poems (page 64)

Eagle, **Peas** and **One, Two** – Anon
Haiku and **Cinquain** – Anon
First verse of **The Stag** by Ted Hughes
Down Behind the Dustbin by Michael Rosen

 ## LESSON ONE

 ## Intended learning

- To explore patterns of rhyme in poetry and to describe how a poet does or does not use rhyme.
- To use patterns to write own poems.

 ## Starting point: Whole class

- Enlarge the poems: 'Eagle', 'Peas', 'Down Behind the Dustbin', 'The Stag' and 'One, Two' (page 64). Tell the children that they are going to share some poems with patterns in them. As you read out the poems, ask the children to think of what the pattern might be.
- Read and discuss each poem again separately. Share any ideas about what the patterns might be. Discuss the following patterns in the poems: 'Down Behind the Dustbin' uses repetition, dialogue, four lines for each verse and lines two and four that rhyme (abcb); 'One, Two' counts consecutively and uses rhyming couplets; 'Eagle' uses rhyme and has the following pattern: 1st line – one word; 2nd line – two words; 3rd line – three words; 4th line – four words; 5th line –

three words; 6th line – two words; 7th line – one word. This poem also has symmetry or a mirror pattern. 'Peas' uses alternate line rhyme (abab) and 'The Stag' is free verse.

- Ask the children if they prefer poems that rhyme. Why/why not? Why do they think a poet may use rhyme? In what way does it help the poem? Why do they think Ted Hughes has not used a pattern or any rhyme in his poem? Does it make the poem more like a story?
- Which pattern used in the poems do the children prefer? Why? Discuss how using a pattern might help the poet write the poem in the first place.
- Explain that they are now going to have a turn at using some patterns to write their own poems. Model how to do each activity before the children begin. The groups could try out each activity or you could assign each group a different task.

 ## Group activities

- Write 'Down Behind the Dustbin' poems by starting each one with:
    Down behind the dustbin
    I met a dog called _____
The children complete the poems by adding two more lines. The last line needs to rhyme with the dog's name.
- Think of words that rhyme with 'two', 'four', 'six', 'eight' and so on and then use these words to make up a new 'One, Two' poem. Encourage the children to use a rhyming dictionary to help them.
- Write poems using the exact pattern of the 'Eagle'.

 ## Plenary session

Bring the whole class together again to share the poems. Ask some children from each group to read out their poems to the others. Do they follow the rules of the pattern? Did the children find it easy to follow a pattern? Does it help them to write a poem more easily? Has it given them some ideas for poetry patterns of their own?

Poems with patterns

 **LESSON TWO** ◆

◆ Intended learning

✦ To recognise simple forms of poetry and their uses.
✦ To explore the use of syllables in poems.
✦ To write own poem.

◆ Starting point: Whole class

✦ Remind the children about the discussion of patterns in poems in Lesson One. What kinds of patterns can they remember?

✦ Tell them that they are going to look at some different patterns in poems; poems that use syllables. Can they tell you what syllables are? Explain the term, likening it to a 'beat' in music. Clap the syllables in some of their names.

✦ Explain that the haiku is a Japanese form of poetry that consists of 17 syllables written in three lines. The first line has 5 syllables, the second 7 and the third 5.

✦ Share the haiku on page 64. Clap out the syllables on each line. Explain that although haiku are only small poems, they still manage to say quite a lot. This is because, when you only have a few words to use, every word counts! Tell them that the whole poem can be used to express an idea, an image or a feeling. Haikus are often used to write about things in nature.

✦ Model writing a haiku together as a class. Think of a subject and brainstorm ideas for each line, agreeing on the most descriptive words to use.

✦ Next, share the cinquain on page 64. How many syllables are there are in each line? Explain that cinquains were invented by an American poet, Adelaide Crapsey. Tell them that the lines can run on from each other and that the last line of two syllables usually makes an impact or statement.

✦ Share the two poems again. Do the children notice anything else? The poems do not rhyme, but have a rhythm due to the pattern of syllables. What do the children think of these types of poems? Would having a syllable pattern help them to write a poem? Tell them that they will now have an opportunity to find out!

◆ Using the differentiated activity sheets

Activity sheet 1

This activity is aimed at children who need more support in writing a haiku. They could work in pairs or small groups to share ideas.

Activity sheet 2

This activity is for more independent workers. They are provided with suggested topics for the poems and are given a framework to follow.

Activity sheet 3

This activity is for more able children. It requires them to write their own haiku and cinquain poems without support.

◆ Plenary session

Bring the whole class together again when the children have completed their poems. Share some from each group. How difficult did they find it to write the poems? Does having a particular pattern to follow help or hinder them? How many different possibilities are there for re-arranging the words on Activity sheet 1? Can others from other groups also suggest alternatives? Discuss how poems can be improved by using a thesaurus to find 'better' or more appropriate words. Ask the children using Activity sheet 3 to comment on how useful they found the thesaurus to be. If time permits, model how to improve one of the poems in this way.

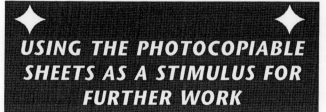

Poems with patterns

USING THE PHOTOCOPIABLE SHEETS AS A STIMULUS FOR FURTHER WORK

✦ Ask the children to write haiku or cinquain poems on a particular theme – perhaps the current class topic. Make a class anthology of the illustrated poems.

✦ Explore other types of syllable poems, such as the tanka, a Japanese form of poetry of 5 lines (5, 7, 5, 7 and 7 syllables).

✦ Challenge the children to use syllable patterns of their own to create rhyming poems. For example, a poem where the last word in each line has two syllables:

> *Cars revving,*
> *bikes zooming,*
> *people talking,*
> *dogs barking,*
> *babies crying,*
> *what a morning!*

✦ Ask the children to search class and library anthologies to find other haiku and cinquain poems. Compare the different approaches to the poems – the subjects used and the effectiveness of the language.

✦ More able children might like to write octosyllabic couplet poems where each line has eight syllables and rhymes in couplets.

✦ Write out other haiku poems with each word on separate pieces of paper as on Activity sheet 1. How many different combinations of the words are possible when they are re-arranged?

OTHER IDEAS FOR USING POEMS WITH PATTERNS

✦ Copy out some rhyming poems, leaving out the last word of the second line in the couplets. Challenge the children to write a word in the spaces so the poem rhymes and makes sense. Roald Dahl's poems from Dirty Beasts and Revolting Rhymes are particularly good to use. For example:

> *No animal is half so vile*
> *As Crocky-Wock the _____*
> *On Saturdays he likes to crunch*
> *Six juicy children for his _____*

✦ Explore rhyme further by looking at poems that have words that rhyme but have different spelling patterns; 'The Ghoul' (page 62) is excellent for this purpose. The children could find words in the poem with the same sound but different spelling patterns (such as 'ghoul' and 'school', 'lungs' and 'tongues' and 'chew' and 'you').

✦ Write poems with patterns using parts of speech. For example:

Noise	*(noun)*
distracting, inescapable	*(2 adjectives)*
disturbs, irritates, angers	*(3 verbs)*
curse of modern times	*(phrase)*
Noise	*(noun)*

✦ Add made-up verses to poems with repeating patterns, such as 'Quartermaster's Stores' (in *A Spider Bought a Bicycle and Other Poems for Young Children* selected by Michael Rosen, Kingfisher Books).

✦ Make up poems where each line begins with the same words. For example:

> *Love is a tender hug*
> *Love is my fluffy cat*
> *Love is my granny's smile*
> *Love is a friendly pat*

◆ Haikus ◆

◆ Complete these haikus by writing suitable words in the spaces. Use a dictionary to help you.

Remember: the first line should have 5 syllables
the second line 7 syllables and
the third line 5 syllables

Raindrops fall like _____
On to the trees _____
Making _____

With his ears _____
The dog _____
Happy to be _____

The sun shines _____
High up _____
Beautiful _____

Autumn leaves fall _____
Brightly coloured _____
What a _____

◆ Now cut out these words. Re-arrange them to make a haiku.

morning	bitter	without
necks	sparrows	together
any	sitting	a

◆ Haikus ◆

◆ Write a haiku by choosing a subject from the word box.
Use the suggestion and a dictionary to help you.

Remember: the first line should have 5 syllables
the second line 7 syllables and
the third line 5 syllables

autumn	sunshine	spring	dog	snow
wind	horse	waves	trees	

Suggestion
First line: What?   (e.g. Huge waves crash loudly)
Second line: Where?   (e.g. On to the sandy shoreline)
Third line: When?   (e.g. Cold winter morning)

◆ Now you try:

What? _____

Where? _____

When? _____

What? _____

Where? _____

When? _____

◆ Haikus and cinquains ◆

✦ Finish the haiku and cinquain below by adding your own lines.
Use a dictionary to help you.

Remember:
A haiku has 3 lines with a syllable pattern of 5, 7 and 5.
A cinquain has 5 lines with a syllable pattern of 2, 4, 6, 8 and 2.

haiku   cinquain

Snowflakes fall softly   Daylight

_____   _____

_____   _____

                                   _____

                                   _____

✦ Now write a haiku and a cinquain of your own on any subject you like.
Use a thesaurus to help you find the most descriptive and expressive
words to use.

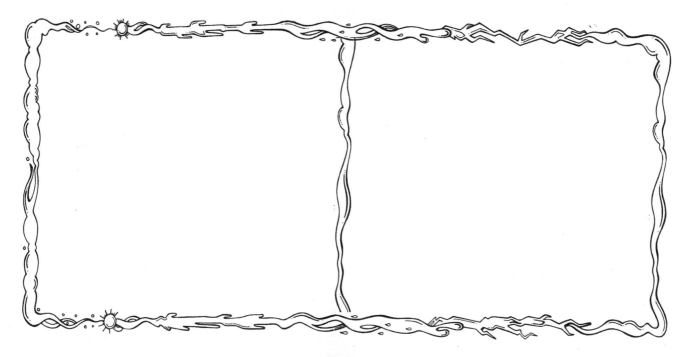

Using Poetry
KS2: Y3–4/P4–5

Developing
literacy
Skills

Photocopiable
© Hopscotch Educational Publishing

55

Winter Morning

Winter is the king of showmen,
Turning tree stumps into snow men
And houses into birthday cakes
And spreading sugar over the lakes.
Smooth and clean and frost white
The world looks good enough to
bite.
That's the season to be young,
Catching snowflakes on your tongue.

Snow is snowy when it's snowing
I'm sorry it's slushy when it's going.

Ogden Nash

Week of Winter Weather

On Monday icy rains poured down
and flooded drains all over town.

Tuesday's gales rent elm and ash;
dead branches came down with a crash.

On Wednesday bursts of hail and sleet;
no one walked along our street.

Thursday stood out clear and calm
but the sun was paler than my arm.

Friday's frost that bit your ears
was cold enough to freeze your tears.

Saturday's sky was ghostly grey;
we smashed ice on the lake today.

Christmas Eve was Sunday and
snow fell like foam across the land.

Wes Magee

Winter

Winter crept
through the whispering wood,
hushing fir and oak;
crushed each leaf and froze each web –
but never a word he spoke.

Winter prowled
by the shivering sea,
lifting sand and stone;
nipped each limpet silently –
and then moved on.

Winter raced
down the frozen stream,
catching at his breath;
on his lips were icicles,
at his back was death.

Judith Nicholls

When Skies are Low and Days are Dark

When skies are low
and days are dark,
and frost bites
like a hungry shark,
when mufflers muffle
ears and nose,
and puffy sparrows
huddle close –
how nice to know
that February
is something purely
temporary.

N M Bodecker

Balloon

```
        a s
      b i g   a s
    ball as round
  as sun . . . I tug
  and pull you when
  you run and when
  wind blows I
      say polite
            ly
            H
            O
            L
            D
            M
            E
            T
            I
            G
            H
            T
            L
            Y.
```

Colleen Thibaudeau

The Snail

behind him a long
silvery trail.
Who leaves
There's none so happy as a garden snail

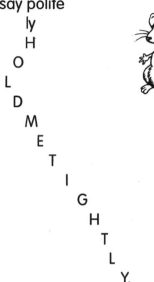

Did you know that the mouse's tail is so very long and thin that when the mouse is out the door his tail is still in ?

Oh   To   Be   a   Hexagon

I wish I wasn't square
With all my sides the same
I'd rather be a triangle
And have an exciting name

I wish I wasn't a square
A square is boring you see
For if I was a hexagon
There'd be lots more sides to me!

TALL, fat and very hairy
The night – time monster is ever so SCARY
He lurks beneath my bed at night
And jumps out suddenly to give me a FRIGHT
But I know the Monster's inside my head
So I close my eyes and snuggle down in bed

Developing Literacy Skills

Photocopiable
© Hopscotch Educational Publishing

Hurricane

Shut the windows
Bolt the doors
Big rain coming
Climbing up the mountain

Neighbours whisper
Dark clouds gather
Big rain coming
Climbing up the mountain

Gather in the clothes lines
Pull down the blinds
Big wind rising
Coming up the mountain

Branches falling
Raindrops flying
Tree tops swaying
People running
Big wind blowing
Hurricane! on the mountain.

Dionne Brand

Roots Man

Some days I dig de groun...Uh-huh
Some days I plant de lan...Uh-huh
Some days I water de crops...Uh-huh
For I am a roots man...Uh-huh

And when de crops produce...Uh-huh
And when I reap de lan...Uh-huh
I know where de goods come from...Uh-huh
For I put in de roots man...Uh-huh

But when I think 'bout this man...Uh-huh
I don't know where I come from...Uh-huh
Some say I am African...Uh-huh
Some say I am Jamaican...Uh-huh

I want to know where I come from...Uh-huh
Does my life have a future plan?...Uh-huh
I want to know who plant this man...Uh-huh
I want to know my roots man!...Uh-huh

Grace Walker Gordon

Childhood Tracks

Eating crisp fried fish with plain bread.
Eating sheared ice made into 'snowball'
with syrup in a glass.
Eating young jelly-coconut, mixed
with village-made wet sugar.
Drinking cool water from a calabash gourd
on worked land in the hills.

Smelling a patch of fermenting pineapples
in stillness of hot sunlight.
Smelling mixed whiffs of fish, mango, coffee,
mint, hanging in a market.
Smelling sweaty padding lifted off a
donkey's back.

Hearing a nightingale in song
in moonlight and sea-sound.
Hearing dawn-crowing of cocks, in answer
to others around the village.
Hearing the laughter
of barefeet children carrying water.
Hearing a distant braying of a donkey
in a silent hot afternoon.
Hearing palmtrees' leaves rattle
on and on at Christmas time.

James Berry

1. The London Bus Conductor's Prayer

Our Father who art in Hendon
Halloway be thy name.
Thy Kingston come,
Thy Wimbledon,
In Erith as it is in Epsom.
Give us this Bray our Maidenhead;
And forgive us our bypasses,
As we forgive those who bypass
against us.
And lead us not into Thames Ditton.
But deliver us from Esher.
For thine is the Kingston,
The Purley and the Crawley,
For Iver and Iver,
Crouch End.

Anon

2. Well, Hardly Ever

Never throw a brick at a drownin' man
Outside a grocery store –
Always throw him a bar of soap –
And he'll wash himself shore.

Anon

3. The Loch Ness Monster's Song

Sssnnnwhufffffll?
Hnwhuffl hhnnwfl hnfl hfl?
Gdroblboblhobngbl gbl gl g g g g glbgl
Drublhaflablhaflubhafgabhaflhafl fl fl –
gm grawwwww grf grawf awfgm graw gm.
Hovoploddok-doplodovok-plovodokot-doplodokosh?
Splagraw fok fok splgrafhatchbagrlgabrl fok splfok!
Zgra kra gka fok!
Grof grawff gahf?
Gombl mbl bl –
blm plm,
blm plm,
blm plm,
blp.

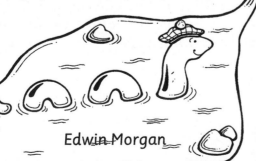

Edwin Morgan

4. Granny

Through every nook and every cranny
The wind blew in on poor old Granny;
Around her knees, into each ear
(And up her nose as well, I fear).

All through the night the wind grew worse,
It nearly made the vicar curse.
The top had fallen off the steeple
Just missing him (and other people).

It blew on man; it blew on beast.
It blew on nun; it blew on priest.
It blew the wig off Auntie Fanny -
But most of all, it blew on Granny!

Spike Milligan

5.

There was a young lady of Lynn,
Who was so uncommonly thin
        That when she essayed
        To drink lemonade,
She slipped through the straw and fell in.

6.

Mary, Mary, quite contrary,
How does your garden grow?
With snails and frogs and neighbours' dogs
And terribly, terribly slow.

Max Fatchen

7. The Optimist

The optimist fell ten storeys
        And at each window bar
He shouted to the folks inside:
        'Doing all right so far!'

Anon

Using Poetry
KS2: Y3–4/P4–5

Developing
Literacy
Skills

Photocopiable
© Hopscotch Educational Publishing

59

Riddles

1.
My first is in feet but not in shoe.
My second is in mince but not in stew.
My third is in sew but not in thread.
My last is in hungry but not in fed.
What am I?

2.
My first is in book but not in cover.
My second is in sister but not in brother.
My third is in rain but not in sun.
My fourth is in bread but not in bun.
What am I?

3.
A house full, a yard full,
And you can't catch a bowl full.

4.
Black within, and red without,
Four corners round about.

5.
What's white and black and red all over?

6.
Why did the roast beef blush?

7.
I'm called by the name of a man,
Yet am as little as a mouse;
When winter comes I love to be
With my red target near the house.

8.
In marble walls as white as milk,
Lined with a skin as soft as silk,
Within a fountain crystal-clear
A golden apple doth appear.
No doors are there to this stronghold,
Yet thieves break in and steal the gold.

No Wonder I Can't Spell!

Learning the English language
Is not something at which I excel.
When so many words sound the same
It's no wonder that I can't spell!

Just look at the words that follow
And I'm sure that you will agree.
There's might and mite, and blue and blew
And flour and flower – do you see?

Which 'to' should I use in a sentence
When there's three different kinds to choose?
And three different 'so's and two different 'dough's;
Do you think it is done to confuse?

Well I think it is time that we changed it
To help other people like me.
Then I can stop worrying about spelling
Oh how wonderful that would be! (or is it bee?)

Frances Mackay

The Sloojee

The Sloojee strikes on nights like this,
When everything is still,
It strikes you if you snore too much,
And makes you feel quite ill.

It makes you cry, it makes you weep,
It makes you mutter in your sleep,
It makes you frown, it makes you fidget,
It makes you wish you were a midget.

It makes you wince, it makes you twice,
It makes your kneecaps turn to ice,
It makes you moan, it makes you wail,
It makes you chew your fingernails.

It makes you scream, it makes you shriek,
It makes you itchy for a week,
It makes you shake, it makes you shiver,
It makes you grateful for your liver.

It makes you spit, it makes you shout,
It makes your teeth and hair fall out,
It makes you twitch, it makes you tremble,
It makes your hip joint reassemble.

The Sloojee strikes, and having struck,
The Sloojee slobbers on,
For when you cease to snore out loud,
It knows its job is done.

Colin West

The Snitterjipe

In mellowy orchards, rich and ripe,
Is found the luminous Snitterjipe.
Bad boys who climb the bulging trees
Feel his sharp breath about their knees;
His trembling whiskers tickle so,
They squeak and squeal till they let go.
They hear his far-from-friendly bark;
They see his eyeballs in the dark
Shining and shifting in their sockets
As round and big as pears in pockets.
They feel his hot and wrinkly hide;
They see his nostrils flaming wide,
His tapering teeth, his jutting jaws,
His tongue, his tail, his twenty claws.
His hairy shadow in the moon
It makes them sweat, it makes them swoon;
And as they climb the orchard wall,
They let their pilfered pippins fall.
The Snitterjipe suspends pursuit
And falls upon the fallen fruit;
And while they flee the monster fierce,
Apples, not boys, his talons pierce.
With thumping hearts they hear him munch—
Six apples at a time he'll crunch.
At length he falls asleep, and they
On tiptoe take their homeward way.
But long before the blackbirds pipe
To welcome day, the Snitterjipe
Has fled afar, and on the green
Only his fearsome prints are seen.

James Reeves

The Ghoul

The gruesome ghoul, the grisly ghoul,
without the slightest noise
waits patiently beside the school
to feast on girls and boys.

He lunges fiercely through the air
as they come out to play,
then grabs a couple by the hair
and drags them far away.

He cracks their bones and snaps their backs
and squeezes out their lungs,
he chews their thumbs like candy snacks
and pulls apart their tongues.

He slices their stomachs and bites their heart
and tears their flesh to shreds,
he swallows their toes like toasted tarts
and gobbles down their heads.

Fingers, elbows, hands and knees
and arms and legs and feet –
he eats them with delight and ease,
for every part's a treat.

And when the gruesome, grisly ghoul
has nothing left to chew,
he hurries to another school
and waits ... perhaps for you.

Jack Prelutsky

The Boodlespook

It's the boodlespook you nincompoop
Of course it's not a dwarf
He's really more than two foot four
But you see he has a stoop
And so would you with three left feet
Two size ten and one size eight
And a pair of arms too short to meet
It's the boodlespook you creep.
It's the boodlespook you utter clot
How can you say you think it's not
What else do you know that's only got
Eleven teeth, with nine on top
And two beneath, but the boodlespook?
It's the boodlespook you barnacle
Of course he wears a monocle
And so would you with just one eye
And that one pointing at the sky
It's the boodlespook you silly chump
It's nothing like a heffalump.
Does a heffalump have turquoise toes
Or a daffodil where its nose should grow
And do heffalumps talk spookabuzz?
Of course they don't, but the boodle does.
It's the boodlespook you drippy wet
I've told you now so don't forget
And if you see him walking by
Don't point or stare or give a cry
Or laugh at him – he's not a fluke
Remember now, he's the boodlespook.

Anon

Developing
literacy
Skills

To a Fish of the Brook

Why flyest thou away with fear?
Trust me there's naught of danger near,
   I have no wicked hook,
All covered with a snaring bait,
Alas, to tempt thee to thy fate,
   And drag thee from the brook.

Enjoy thy stream, O harmless fish;
And when an angler for his dish,
   Through gluttony's vile sin,
Attempts, a wretch, to pull thee *out*,
God give thee strength, O gentle trout,
   To pull the rascal *in!*

John Walcot

The Fly

How large unto the tiny fly
Must little things appear!
– A rosebud like a feather bed,
Its prickle like a spear,
A dewdrop like a looking-glass
A hair like golden wire;
The smallest grain of mustard-seed
As fierce as coals of fire;
A loaf of bread, a lofty hill;
A wasp, a cruel leopard;
And specks of salt as bright to see
As lambkins to a shepherd.

Walter de la Mare

Sweet Suffolk Owl

Sweet Suffolk Owl, so trimly dight
With feathers, like a lady bright,
Thou sing'st alone, sitting by night,
   Te whit! Te whoo! Te whit! Te whoo!

Thy note that forth so freely rolls
With shrill command the mouse controls;
And sings a dirge for dying souls –
   Te whit! Te whoo! Te whit! Te whoo!

Thomas Vautor

Upon the Snail

She goes but softly, but she goeth sure;
She stumbles not as stronger creatures do;
Her journey's shorter, so she may endure
Better than they which do much further go.

She makes no noise, but stilly seizeth on
The flower or herb appointed for her food
The which she quietly doth feed upon,
While others range and gare, but find no
   good.

And though she doth but very softly go,
However 'tis not fast, not slow, but sure;
And certainly they that do travel so,
The prize they do aim at, they do procure.

John Bunyan

One, Two

One, two,
Buckle my shoe;
Three, four,
Knock at the door;
Five, six,
Pick up sticks;
Seven, eight,
Lay them straight;
Nine, ten,
A good fat hen.

Eagle
with huge
talons that claw,
wings that fiercely beat
above the wide
forest floor
Eagle

Peas

I eat my peas with honey,
I've done it all my life,
They do taste kind of funny,
But it keeps them on the knife.

from: **The Stag**

While the rain fell on the November woodland shoulder of
    Exmoor
While the traffic jam along the road honked and shouted
Because the farmers were parking wherever they could
And scrambling to the bank-top to stare through the
    tree-fringe
Which was leafless,
The stag ran through his private forest.   **Ted Hughes**

Haiku
Snowflakes falling down
In a whirl of dancing glee
Cold ballerinas

Cinquain
Sunshine
Warms the heavens.
Rays of golden splendour
Brighten our day, give us life and
Vision.

Down behind the dustbin

Down behind the dustbin
I met a dog called Ted.
'Leave me alone,' he says,
'I'm just going to bed.'

Down behind the dustbin
I met a dog called Felicity.
'It's a bit dark here,' she said,
'They've cut off the electricity.'

Down behind the dustbin
I met a dog called Roger.
'Do you own this bin?' I said.
'No. I'm only the lodger.'

Ian said,
Down behind the dustbin
I met a dog called Sue.
'What are you doing here?' I said.
'I've got nothing else to do.'

Down behind the dustbin
I met a dog called Anne.
'I'm just off now,' she said,
'to see a dog about a man.'

Down behind the dustbin
I met a dog called Jack.
'Are you going anywhere?' I said.
'No. I'm just coming back.'

Down behind the dustbin
I met a dog called Billy.
'I'm not talking to you,' I said,
'if you're going to be silly.'

Down behind the dustbin
I met a dog called Barry.
He tried to take the bin away
but it was too heavy to carry.

Down behind the dustbin
I met a dog called Mary.
'I wish I wasn't a dog,' she said,
'I wish I was a canary.'

                              Michael Rosen

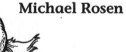

Developing
literacy
Skills